ANOTHER WRINKLE IN TIME

The Art Of Aging

Robert Faber

iUniverse LLC
Bloomington

ANOTHER WRINKLE IN TIME
The Art Of Aging

iUniverse books may be ordered through booksellers or by contacting:

iUniverse LLC
1663 Liberty Drive
Bloomington, IN 47403
www.iuniverse.com
1-800-Authors (1-800-288-4677)

ISBN: 978-1-4759-2532-6 (sc)
ISBN: 978-1-4759-2533-3 (hc)
ISBN: 978-1-4759-2534-0 (e)

Library of Congress Control Number: 2012908146

Printed in the United States of America

iUniverse rev. date: 10/12/2013

Contents

Introduction

As seniors, much of who we now are was determined by our genes and that was further aided or thwarted by the good- or ill-fortune that directed us during our more formative early years. But now, reflecting on our lengthening past, we find that it was more likely the impact of the experiences that faced us and shaped us as we matured that should be given the major role on center stage.

That long transition from Youngster to Senior continuously burdened us with new problems to resolve, new goals to pursue, new responsibilities to confront, so that much of our time and energy was devoted to dealing with conditions on the ground or some of those still facing us. However, upon reaching retirement—that period past our child-parent-responsibility years and beyond our accumulating-more-funds-for-old-age years—preparation for the challenges of each new tomorrow lost its urgency. The quality of our future is no longer dependent on anticipating all the many hurdles that might face us in order to better meet them. Because we must no longer predict the next turn in the road, we tend to bypass most of the looming uncertainties and simply sit back and relax.

And that could be a formula for personal disaster.

Aristotle's observation that "Nature abhors a vacuum" was not meant as a critique of Man, but for most seniors such an application is well targeted. The vacuum generated within ourselves by the lethargy common to old age—the empty hours, the blank schedules, the limited interests and responsibilities—is as abhorrent to us as it is to Nature and as destructive. It, too, should be examined, understood and treated. The role we seniors had played as responsible adults in protecting our families and building our futures is now outdated, but the procedure should not simply be abandoned because of the reduced resources or more limited skills of age. The alternative, just sitting around waiting for things to happen, feeds the shortcomings of Age and can hasten our deterioration.

Very simply, at whatever age and burdened with whatever physical obstacles, we must continue to participate. Even when losing control of some of the more common and basic ingredients of our life, we must play the game as if we count. It is not the product, after all, but the process, the challenge itself that can strengthen our physical and psychological selves and that is the pivotal factor in our late years. And, too, of course, the fact is that we do still count. The experiences we encountered during our journey have given us some valuable insights, a better understanding of some of the ways of the world that may be worth passing on to those still trying to catch up. Our accumulated experiences have have provided us with enough information to benefit at least some members of the emerging generations—and that alone would be a reassuring justification for ourselves, for the time we have already spent on the trip.

And even if we are not successful in our senior efforts at building or doing or teaching, the satisfaction in continuing to push ourselves with as much energy and enthusiasm as we are able to go as far as we reasonably can is enough to justify whatever time and thought we had put into it. For our senior years, after all, it is as much the gratification of having tried hard and done well that is the reward of the extended buildup. Ultimately, it is more the hope and the anticipation of success that drives us than it is the the rewards of the triumph itself.

The chapters in this book originated in *The Ann Arbor News* as articles of advice for seniors on how to fill the empty spaces in lives made increasingly low on plan or purpose because of the accumulation of years. It is my hope that this effort might help emerging seniors better understand and more effectively deal with some of the pleasures and pitfalls of age and of the aging process and perhaps to be energized by the challenges of the years remaining in this new phase of life.

In short, the purpose of this collection of articles is not to analyze or dwell on the accumulation of years past, but to encourage a concentration on enhancing the quality of those yet remaining. Senior status, after all, need not be just the beginning of an end, but may well be judged and enjoyed as simply the next phase in our lives—and perhaps prove to be a productive and pleasurable one as well.

Bob Faber

The Bottom Line

S ome wise old character once observed that the principal objection to old age is that there is no future in it. Most members of the tribe of elders can suggest a few additions to that single-segment list of objections, but few serious enough to devalue the many treats still available in that late phase. The pitfalls of aging may be enough to crush its pleasures—but only if we let them. The downside of age-related deterioration is painfully clear, but concentration on its shortcomings serves no purpose.

"Old" is not new, but getting older—much older—is becoming ever more common. At the turn of the 20th century, for example, 4 percent of our people were sixty-five years and older. Now that number has more than tripled—to 13 percent. That's the good news. The more troubling concern is how we old-folk are handling that emerging longevity.

Having done our job and done it well is a worthy legacy, but may not be enough to end our journey with a full sense of pleasure and pride. My own choice, not universally available but preferable when possible, is to continue the search or the fight or the game well into the future, however limited or problematic that future may be. The disabilities waiting around our corner are too distressing and too well known to list, but to rest on the past and agonize over trauma that are still only pending is an excellent way to waste valuable and increasingly scarce time. However satisfying the past may have been, it is still the past. What is needed closer to the end is something to fill the empty space of inactivity.

The Greek poet Homer, writing about Ulysses, the hero of the Trojan War, ended his tale with the great warrior at home with his wife, living in peace and prosperity. To most of us that may sound like a pretty good conclusion, but the poet Tennyson felt otherwise about Ulysses' retirement:

> How dull it is to pause, to make an end,
> To rust unburnished, not to shine in use!
> As though to breath were life!

And that is the point about the tail end of life's adventures. If the end of the tale leaves nothing but memories and an empty schedule, it's time to explore new directions, new adventures. The vacuum at the end of the process can be more agonizing than restful, so we should not quit.

To lend credibility to some of my amateur conclusions I find support in the works of the University of Michigan's Dr. Robert Kahn, Professor of Psychology and of Public Health, whose book "Successful Aging" examines some of those same issues, albeit more thoroughly and much more professionally. He notes, for example, that for the past several decades the practice of gerontology was preoccupied more with the problems of disability and disease than with the positive aspects of aging. The new goal of today's gerontologists, however, is to look beyond the limited view of chronological age and to emphasize the positive aspects of aging, or as Dr. Kahn puts it, "to find the difference between putting one octogenarian in a wheelchair and another on cross-country skis."

Dr. Kahn then adds, "Most people seem to feel that how well one ages is hereditary, [but] . . . environment and lifestyle may be more important." He notes that while much of all mental loss connected with age is genetic, "the other half is related to lifestyle and environment. In other words, there is a lot one can do to keep one's mind sharp with age." Very simply, exercise of any sort—whether physical or mental—is valuable and productive. (In one of his successful experiments he initiated an exercise class in a nursing home. The class dealt with a wide variety of exercises, including weightlifting, and a wide range of aged participants, including a woman ninety-eight years old. They all took part and they all improved.) He then concluded, "There is a simple, basic fact about exercise and your health: fitness cuts your risk of dying. It doesn't get much more 'bottom line' than that."

That doesn't work for all of us, of course. Much is determined by our personal characteristics, by who we are and how we handled the earlier days of our growth. And that is the key to rekindling our enthusiasm—go light on the "still pending" downsides of the future and stay positive by actively planning and working for tomorrow.

In brief, it is activity that keeps us active. And it is the anticipation of that activity that keeps us interested. And it is that interest in the variables and challenges of the future that spark our later years. And all of that gives it a firm place in Dr. Kahn's "bottom line."

Election Fever . . . Part Of The Game

Now that we've grown older and can see things in the light of real life experiences, we understand that the reality of politics is nothing like they taught us in school, so perhaps we should change some of the rules of the game.

And it is a game, so perhaps the list of candidates for the next election should include some of the giants in games, like LeBron James of basketball, or Peyton Manning of football, or Tiger Woods of golf. Those guys may know nothing about government or economics, but they look great, are comfortable with the press, are widely known and well liked, and have annual incomes in the millions—all the attributes necessary for seeking a place in Washington. Their athletic skills may have no application in running the country, but that is an increasingly fringe requirement for election to high office.

And that is the essence of our growing national tragedy. Our choice for leadership has come to rely much more extensively on posturing on television and proclaiming wisdom with sound-bite clichés than on serious and objective analysis. And that is not what our government had been or who we are. At its inception the Constitution swore to "form a more perfect Union, establish Justice, . . . promote the general Welfare, and secure the Blessings of Liberty"—a pledge unique in the history of nations. Unfortunately, that noble goal is ill served by aggressive political attacks designed solely to denigrate the opposition. Showmanship to win elections is a reasonable and acceptable part of the game, but offered in lieu of productive discussion diminishes the higher principles of governance, ultimately damaging the value and integrity of the system.

Throughout our history we have been blessed with a variety of strong, wise and committed legislative leaders who were able to calm the passions of disagreement and to work with their opposition. That group is now in increasingly short supply. The honor of legislative service that had once been its own reward has since adjusted to the pleasures of position and the perks of power.

Designated by the Constitution as the first branch of government, the Congress is known as "the world's greatest deliberative body," a description unfortunately at odds with its new reality. According to Norman Ornstein in "The Broken Branch," it has assumed the new label of "The Tuesday-to-Thursday Club," its members "straggling in late on Tuesday then get[ting] out of town as early on Thursday as possible," leaving no time for the productive discussions that come from personal relationships with members of the opposition. Replacing those searching and frequently productive discussions are the vitriolic attacks taking place on the floor of Congress and generally as the focus of the television news—our nation's primary new entertainment,

Whatever distance now separates us from the intent of our Constitution, its principles remain a treasured part of our heritage and the presumed definition of our values. And if that noble heritage is really a myth, it is *our* myth, venerated by *our* people and now an essential part of who we like to believe we are. The Constitution's homage to the "the welfare of the People" is disappearing from our political horizon and victim of the exigencies of "practical politics." Submission to the dictates of Party, determined by the demands of financial or ideological backers may win elections, but they profane our principles, leaving a leadership more beholden to its patrons than to its people.

The problem is clear—the solution much less so. Ornstein attributes much of the fault to the collapse of Congressional responsibility, its loss of independence as the oversight branch of government. He sees "a legislative process that has lost the transparency, accountability, and deliberation that are at the core of the American system."

However accurate his diagnosis, there must be a higher standard of integrity for those to whom we entrust the mechanics and future of our nation. The sacred ideals and traditions by which our people and our nation are defined are colliding with the reality of power politics and political greed. Satisfying the needs of the many over the preferences of a privileged and powerful few has been our national ideal, but that condition cannot exist in today's environment.

The promises written in our Constitution and the plea articulated on our Statue of Liberty to *"Give me your tired, your poor, your huddled masses yearning to breathe free"* define our nation's character and its goals. And even if we too often fall short, to our credit we have retained and honored the spirit of those aspirations. Clearly the needy and afflicted international communities cannot be our nation's primary obligation, but our loss as an inspiration for those oppressed populations is a troubling reflection of how we are faring at home with our *own* people and *their* dreams.

We seniors have spent the better part of a century pursuing the narrow agenda of improving life for ourselves and our progeny. It is time for our candidates to drop their "TV game show" electioneering and aim higher than the personal glories of the moment. The principles of the Constitution started our nation on its journey—they should now be the goal and the measurement of our performance.

The Flexible Rules Of Aging

For bending the curve of a soccer ball in flight, check with Beckham—he's the guy who wrote the book. And with questions about electronic technologies, go to Steve Jobs, for whom the computer was the Apple of his eye. And for advice on making fortunes out of thin air, there's Bernie Madoff. The world is full of experts, but for handling the problems of growing old you're on your own.

To a large extent "old age" is primarily a highly personal series of reactions to the incidentals of growing old. The experiences accumulated during the journey, influenced by a genetic code beyond our comprehension or control, are generally the end product of a luck and fate that plays games with our minds and bodies. And even for those of us fortunate enough to be reasonably free of the debilitating downsides of ill health or poverty, old age is largely a residue of frustrations or disappointments or disillusions that had cast shadows over our remaining days.

But neither those experiences nor their consequences need necessarily be negative. As a fairly aggressive optimist, I had always pursued life's tasks with a respectable degree of work and diligence, but my natural (too often irrational) optimism protected me from despair. Coming up short never really worried me because of my unreasonable confidence in the good fortunes of the morrow. It has recently struck me, however, that I have just about run out of morrows. From childhood through middle-age I leaned heavily on daydreams, finding success and reassurance in fantasy, a satisfying compensation for whatever real or imagined inadequacies were then bedeviling me. My athletic achievements, my amorous conquests, my youthful military derring-do—they were all great moments yet to come. With age my dreams matured. Next year will be better—I'll win the election to (whatever), or a large firm will buy my business and make me their chief something or other, or my carefully selected lottery numbers will come together for The Grand Prize. Well, I'm not running for office, and I no longer have a business to sell, and at 84 no firm is likely to hire me except as a "greeter" of customers at Walmart's, and my investments in the Lottery sadly mirror my investments in the stock market. Stardom, heroism and Don Juanism have long since passed me by. It is increasingly evident that I'll not make it (whatever that elusive "it" may be) and that in turn prompts much of my discomfort and displeasure with the approaching state of Old Age. My blind, irrational, but comforting belief that it will all come together "down the road" has deserted me: I'm running out of road.

And therein lies the problem—the conflict between the good and the bad of my natural optimism. My early and middle years enjoyed welcome support in the anticipated successes of the future. Old Age, on the other hand, is characterized by the unfamiliar realization that tomorrow is simply the day after today. I have always waited with a joyful anticipation of the news the next day might bring—my article will be published (they seldom were); my investments would suddenly take off (they never did); I would be approached to participate in some rosy new venture (I was never on anybody's list). I've not been trained for reality. At 84 I still think of "old age" as some feature of the distant future. Without tomorrow how can I handle the shortcomings of today?

I think of my friend who had long nursed a secret dream of being on Michigan's State Supreme Court. As a politically active and inspired lawyer, he had long been involved on the fringes of politics, but now, on his mid-life birthday, he was struck with the realization that such an appointment would never be his—a suspicion long assumed, but now accepted as fact. But such disappointments, while common, need not be definitive. In his case, after coming to terms with reality, he simply changed his goals to more plausible possibilities and built a bright future on a smaller scale.

And that seems to be one of the great overlooked secrets: dream, and dream big, but don't aim so irrationally high that falling short can be too bitter a disappointment. Better to be thrilled with more modest accomplishments. My articles may yet be published, and my new putting grip makes it certain that I'll break a hundred, and my stocks—while now worth a fraction of their cost—may yet be discovered and coveted by Warren Buffett.

My wife cautions that I have been irrationally positive about the future for longer than the past half-century, but that caution comes too late—my path has long been set and my flaws ingrained. That "blind hope" for the future has grown into a certainty of satisfaction—that the market will indeed escalate and that my golf ball will finally find its hole and that the sky's gloom of grey will brighten into an inspiring shad of pink.

Optimism is not a characteristic that can readily be turned on and off—and it certainly does not yield to logic—but it can do quite a bit to relieve much of the anguish of reality.

Gaining Expertise: It Takes Time

Old age is more than just a waiting room for the last act—it can also be a setting for rejuvenation. As a personal example: after eight decades of searching for that particular set of skills or deeds that might mark my place in the world, I have finally found it as an Octogenarian—I am now a member of the Class Of The Pretty Old.

But it did not come quickly or without a struggle.

World War II offered me the promise of heroism, the chance to distinguish myself on the nation's field of honor. Only trouble was that I was born just a bit too late. By leaving the womb a year earlier I could have helped thwart the German offensive in Europe or supported our invading forces in the Pacific, but I was just a bit too young. On my seventeenth birthday I joined the Army Air Corps with dreams of glory, only to discover that because of my age I was limited to the newly formed Army Air Corps *Reserves,* which meant I wouldn't be called up until I turned eighteen (I've never been good with details). A year later I was allowed to begin my service and go through basic training, but before releasing me into the Wild Blue Yonder, my time ran out, the war ran out, and I was sent home.

I then moved to Ann Arbor and opened a fabric store, but my dreams needed more, so I got involved in local politics and ran for City Council—twice—and failed—twice. A few years later I tried again and made it—just in time to be buffeted by the revolutionary tactics of the "sixties" generation, one of the more raucous and challenging periods in our city's history. After two terms of confrontation, of bluster and experiment and finally of compromise and growth, peace returned to the community and I returned to my business.

Unfortunately, during those few years of service my small world of business had changed. Women were now working more and sewing less and no longer needed me or my product, so I closed my fabric stores and tried my hand in an entirely different field. I opened a travel agency, but that, too, was soon warped by a new technology. Most of our potential travel clients—students and faculty at the University—now had their own computers and and computer skills and no longer needed travel agents to find and book their flights, so my business and I were soon surplus. (The resultant fantasy was that in the name of world peace I should get into the munitions business—then there would be no more war.) Finally, having learned, practiced and succeeded in separate fields joined only by their obsolescence, what's left for a future?

Plenty—which is the point of this long discourse. Life's defining moments can be difficult to pinpoint—the first day of school? the first amorous relationship? the first job—but the common thread is the discovery of new horizons to explore and new challenges to overcome. We may have traveled this road before and succeeded or failed in our several endeavors, but there are still other paths to consider. If a new direction in life is the fuel that moves us forward, that can be as readily available and as richly rewarding for the old as it was for the young. Even in our seventies and beyond there is always something more that we have not yet tried. And if we try and fail? So what. It's the pursuit that is the prize, more the thrill of the race than the trophy.

For myself, as an example, having long been immersed in business, it was time to try something new. Writing had always held a special appeal for me, but with no particular field of expertise to build a case, or explore a theory or with which to express myself, I was little more than an interloper. I knew a little about some of life's challenges, but except for escaping obsolete retail and travel businesses I had no documented expertise, no credentials in any of the fields about which I would write.

Which is part of my message. Aging has its many drawbacks, but even aside from its preference to the alternative, the simple fact of survival provides a verifiable expertise. For me, that is one of the values of Aging—at last I'm an expert! Upon his retirement, the president can write about his political experiences—he knows his subject. And the firefighter who survived 9/11 can write about the drama and tragedies of that crisis—he's been there. And now, finally, I too am an expert. I can write about some of the fears and follies, some of the highlights and low moments of Age and Aging. I'm a member. I've been there. I am there. Maybe "expert" is a bit too grand, but now what I write is either good or it's garbage, but it can no longer be dismissed as the empty thoughts of an amateur on the outside looking in. True, I have no degree to back my claim of experience or expertise, but I do have a very old birth certificate and that should give me at least some degree of authenticity.

So whether looking forward or back, whether anticipating what may still lie ahead or reminiscing about what has gone before, the aging process still has a lot to recommend it. It may not have much of a future, but what is left can be satisfying—and sometimes even productive.

Guided By Principles

As seniors who came on the scene during the later moments of the Great Depression, we like to think we have learned our lessons and that the horrors of those years are gone. Unfortunately, one of our more disturbing lessons is that we tend to forget more quickly than we learn and that the misery of that period, if not forgotten, remains in our memory as an abstraction, without reality or pain.

Today, overcoming the trauma of our economic adversity is among our top priorities—creating more jobs and reducing our national debt—but topping even that goal is the necessity of doing so without increasing taxes.

The dispute has little to do with the principle of helping the needy—no one objects to that—but has everything to do with how we're going to pay for it. The national obsession with taxes has convinced much of the population that "we're trying to do too much too soon—we should wait until we can better afford it, wait until the economy improves." The trouble with such a delay is that for the terminally ill, or those about to lose their home, or for children just starting out with Head Start, there may be no "long-term." The admonition of the Constitution to "promote the general welfare" says nothing about adjusting that responsibility when inconvenient.

That same paragraph refers to "provid[ing] for the common defense," so after the attack of 9/11 we responded by attacking Afghanistan, thus beginning the Gulf War. But there was no cost analysis made preceding that action—we just did it. Some obligations of government are simply obligations of government and whatever the pain or inconvenience, they must be borne. It is that selfless commitment to the welfare of the nation—to its economy and its infrastructure, but equally to its voiceless, powerless poor—that has distinguished our country from all others since it first took form over two centuries ago. Legislators' concentration on taxes makes sense for reelection, but is a serious departure from its constitutional responsibilities.

Concern about our nation's economic well-being is a necessary caution, but positioning the displeasure of paying taxes ahead of matters of survival for major segments of our population is damaging to those principles that distinguish our nation from all others. Unfortunately and unfairly, it is those who are least benefited by the disputed tax cuts who must now bear the burden of our fiscal adjustments. Trying to balance our budget by reducing subsidies for welfare services is essentially a program of levying a tax on the nation's most disadvantaged. Keeping within the parameters of our Constitution's pledge to "promote the general Welfare" suggests that we first decide what is needed and proper for our people, *then* how best to pay for it. It is simply a matter of priorities.

And that is the problem—whose priorities? A gored ox for one may be a grand opportunity for another. The real issue is how our national priorities are set and by what guidelines? By logic and tradition, reliance on the Constitution, the revered articulation of the hopes and aspirations of the Founders, has served our nation well. We all want the best, most trouble-free life possible, but if our individual comfort and security is achieved at the expense of our fellows' misery, then our focus needs revision. Our destination and the route to its fulfillment should be set by principles rather than by voter appeal or the demands of our population's more powerful constituents. The principles of our Constitution are a wonderful guide for legislative performance, and if its benefits are not immediately available within the limitations of the existing budget—revise the budget, not the principles.

Admittedly that will be a formidable task. Many of our citizens have worked hard and honorably to improve their lifestyle and secure their well-being. They are reasonably entitled to the benefits of their efforts and to view as unfair the taxing of those benefits in order to help those whose work habits or skills are of a lower order. But that must not be the end of it. The principled demands of our Constitution are not empty clichés, but are the bedrock of our society, the face and traditions that we present to the world and that we like to believe define our people.

Our nation's finances are strained, but rather than adjusting our goals to fit the convenience of our resources, we should concentrate on the problems to be fixed. Legislative decisions should be based on protecting and improving our entire society—not on the temporary inconvenience of economic setbacks. As a general principle advocated by FDR, our nation's basic responsibility includes feeding the hungry and clothing the naked and sheltering the homeless. Sacrifices in difficult times must be borne by *all* our people—not by those least equipped to cope. We are more than just another country in which everyone struggles and competes and the losers simply lose. In his second inaugural address in 1937, Franklin Roosevelt said, "Government is competent when all who compose it work as trustees for the whole people."

Not a bad definition of principles by which to govern . . . and to live.

Keeping Our Place In The World

They came here as the 19th century gave way to the 20th. They had little in common beyond their shared poverty and their desperation . . . and a naive hope that somehow things would be better in this new land of promise.

The plea of the welcoming Statue in the New York harbor to *"Give me your tired, your poor, your huddled masses yearning to breathe free"* resonated with oppressed and despairing people around the world, giving them hope for a life that might include security and liberty and a chance to earn a modest living. And it succeeded— giving them all of that and more. It gave them the hope and dignity and promise of a life that, within the limits of luck and personal skills, offered the fulfillment of all the many dreams that had first tempted them to make that hazardous trip into the unknown.

And for many it worked as advertised. From my youth, for example, in the early days of World War II, I remember meeting the young peddler, a poor and recent refugee from the hopeless depths of discrimination and despair of Lithuania, who worked around the clock, selling linings to fabric stores from the trunk of his battered old jalopy, trying to support his small family. When I met him again some years later he had graduated to working out of a loft in the fabric district in New York where he proudly showed me the picture of his son, The Doctor. Only in America!

A century has passed since those "poor [and] huddled masses" sought and found their dream in America, but for today's distant victims of despair, that dream is beginning to fade, the casualty of a narrowing vision increasingly focused on purely partisan politics and personal gain. That promise of a new beginning is becoming less likely, less inviting—and our nation and the world are the poorer for it. It is not our national responsibility to serve the afflicted nations of the world, but the sense of justice embedded in our constitution that had so inspired the rest of the world and excited such a reassuring sense of pride within our nation and among ourselves is rapidly losing substance—and the fading light of that national benevolence should trouble us all. We are fast becoming just another nation, measuring our status and progress by economic advances rather than the success of our revered constitutional principles of "promot[ing] the general Welfare."

The most immediate example of our social decline is in the attitudes attacking the issue of universal healthcare. Unlike FDR's observation that *"[The nation] cannot be content ... if some fraction of our people is ill fed, ill-clothed, ill-housed, and insecure,"* our recent dispute centered on the tax burdens of charity, or the inconvenience that might accrue to private industry, or the fear of some future shift of responsibility from corporate power to government control. Those concerns are not invalid, but our concentration should be focused much more firmly on the needs of our people, on the *principles* expressed by our founding documents, rather than on the *tactics* of implementation.

Some issues dividing our nation are significant and profound and may well be insoluble except by compromise—such as the opposing views on abortion, or the right to voluntarily end one's own life of irredeemable pain and suffering, or the legal sanctification of same-sex marriage—but our heritage demands more than personal or ideological victories. Legislative decisions must be measured by what they bring to the whole people. A concentration on tax cuts, for example, must be weighed against the loss of valued social programs funded by those missing tax dollars. The *ethics* of governance are being replaced by the *tactics* of control—at a cost of the principles by

17

which our nation is defined. We have been taught—by our schools, by our traditions, by our love and respect for our history—that the United States is the most caring, compassionate and supportive nation in the world. And we probably are. The richness of our democracy, after all, is not in doubt, only its ownership, so tax relief for the wealthy continues to take congressional precedence over Head Start.

Meanwhile, the sacred ideals and traditions by which our people and our nation are defined is colliding with the reality of power politics and political greed. The dollars needed to care for our people are jeopardized by programs of narrowly applied tax relief and the demands of the larger political contributors. Employing political tactics to accomplish self-serving ends is hardly a new technique, but the idealism which has so long been our guide and our pride must not be sacrificed in the process. Satisfying the needs of the many over the preferences of the privileged and powerful few must remain our national ideal.

And lest FDR's message be dismissed as the oratory of a "godless Liberal," consider the admonition of Deuteronomy 15: 7-8: "When there is among you a needy person . . . you are to open . . . your hand to him and are to . . . pledge to him sufficient for his lack that is lacking to him."

From Amateur To Expert:
Closing The Gap

I am *not* the world's worst athlete—just a slow learner.

Golf is a good example of my predicament. True, I've been playing for almost seventy years, but I've not been really serious about the game until the last few decades. Now I can fully understand those small details that spell the difference between rank amateurism and budding mediocrity. Now that I'm about to break a hundred (really, I'm right on the edge) I can attribute the improvement to a better understanding of all those many details that come with age and practice. I've increased my pivot, loosened my putting grip and learned to keep my eye on the ball. I know, doesn't sound like much, but it makes all the difference in my game. It's not just the strength of the player, after all, or the natural grace with which he/she might be blessed, or even the size of the bet that's been wagered during an explosive outburst of frustration triggered by a long series of losses. It's the calm application of science—and the patience that comes with age—that separates winners from losers in the world of golf. But as I said, I'm a slow learner.

My tennis falls into roughly the same category of moving slowly from totally inadequate to increasingly nearly adequate. I play in a senior men's tennis game with a bunch of youngsters in their sixties and seventies, and except for my exhaustion half way through the game I can now hold my own reasonably well. When I joined the game a few years ago I was the weakest player of the group, but after calmly analyzing my game and the science of returning the ball to the other side of the net, I've learned the basic rudiments of the game and am much less embarrassed—even if rarely proud. Once again the secret is in the science, understanding the relationship between the ball and the racquet and the boundaries of the court—and myself. (I throw myself into this equation because anxiety to make up for my inadequacy prompts me to run full speed after anything that falls on my side of the net, so that half way through our two-hour game I'm very near collapse.) But here again, it's the game's scientific approach that brought me to where I am and gives me hope for the future.

And it's not in just those course and court-side athletic activities that my new skills and higher quality performances are revealed I started skiing in college untold decades ago, but I was a bit lacking in grace and style. My roommate, already familiar with the sport and reasonably accomplished, helped me up the lower slope of a mountain in New Hampshire, turned me away from its face and toward the world—and gave me a shove. The bottom of that run was separated from the parking lot by a row of steel posts, so without any understanding of how to turn or stop I had no alternative to self-destruction other than to fall on my face just short of the divide. For three days I went up the mountain, came down the mountain, and bounced on my face to stop at the bottom of the mountain. My most impressive accomplishment during that three-day ordeal was survival, but hey, that counts for something.

But then I got married, had children and became a caring and devoted father—a classification that included taking my children to Boyne Mountain, a ski resort in northern Michigan. Problem was that my ski skills were not much improved from those early days of disaster, whereas my older, pre-teen son was a natural who disappeared after breakfast each morning and returned for dinner—with a full day's skiing behind him and a new set of skills supporting him. The intervening years of clash between his grace on the slopes and my inadequacy can be better understood by the advice he offered me much later in our ski life: "Look, dad, when you're coming down a steep slope with a lot of moguls, you've gotta take each mogul one at a time. Just bounce off the one in front of you, make your turn, then bounce again off the next one. That way you can keep on bouncing and turning all the way down and build up some great speed. It's easy." It wasn't easy. What turned out to be easy was growing older and less competitive and waiting for the new style of skis to come out—the shorter parabolic skis designed to stroke the ego of aging non-athletes.

The other change that made skiing easier was competing less with my children and more with my very young grandchildren, whom I've brainwashed into thinking me really talented and attributing my slow speed to my desire to stay with them. But even this has a downside. They're growing older and are increasingly aware of their grandfather's shortcomings. But hope for the future remains. Some of my grandchildren are nearing the age of marriage, so maybe I'll have a chance to impress another generation.

And therein lies another benefit of aging: learning that falling short of perfection—or even of adequacy—can be just as valuable and satisfying as winning. As with most efforts, doing our best with what we've got—and enjoying the experience—is often enough to define victory.

Looking Forward

About almost everything, we have choices. We can ignore them or use them or abuse them—and that's another choice that is ours to make. One of our choices is in the examination and interpretation of times both past and anticipated, but however we handle it, just having that choice is a precious power that should not be wasted.

For seniors, the anticipation of looking forward—to the next event or the next challenge or simply the next Tomorrow—is part of what gives us the interest and suspense to keep us connected to the moment. And it is that stimulus that helps us overcome some of the less pleasant, more unsettling realities of Today. And it is the choice we then make, whether looking forward or evaluating the past, that adds to the control we may still have over our lives.

When we were slightly younger the variables of the coming days were mostly determined by the obligations of parenthood and wage-earning. Now, having advanced into old age, dealing with the facts and incidentals of Tomorrow becomes less a restriction and assumes more the glow of salvation, the chance to escape or ignore some of our limitations rather than to be inhibited by them. Looking forward to identify and perhaps deal with the mysteries still ahead can keep us focused with interest and suspense on the future—an increasingly rare and satisfying activity for seniors.

But of course, that does not free us of what had gone before, or of its consequences. As seniors, one of our special privileges is the opportunity to look back at some of the moments of our distant youth and adjust them to better fit the contours we had originally assigned them, thereby supporting our magnified view of ourselves.

From my own inventory of memories, for example, I recall my time as an eighth grade student at a school bordering the Delaware River in Trenton and walking part way to Philadelphia atop the frozen blocks of its midwinter, ice-jammed surface. In retrospect, of course, trying to stay balanced on its slippery, steeply-angled, massive chunks of ice, ignoring the crushed legs or drowning promised by a careless misstep, was much more a sign of juvenile foolishness, perhaps idiocy, than of courage, but clarity of thought was not my teenage strength.

It is now over seventy years since that inglorious conquest and still it brings a touch of satisfaction to my hungry ego—which is the pleasure of memories long since developed. But the joys of revisiting the past need not go all the way back to childhood. There are many moments along the path to maturity that can still add color and bring satisfaction to what may really have been fairly bland, mid-life activities—and these, too, should be examined and embraced for how they may stimulate our memories. Too many seniors, without the demands of the old job and without the skills to be confident in pursuing new activities, just settle for the life of the moment—going to the movies, reading a book, watching TV—all of which are fine, but inadequate. There is often too little search for something more. The careful use, perhaps even manipulation, of memorable moments from our past can provide benefits useful in expanding the lives we now live, even adding some interest and satisfaction to the moment.

If distant memories can be seen as part of our inventory, they can also be used as an asset. By recording the events of those ancient days we are building a history for those of our family who follow, meanwhile bringing more structure and interest to the days we now fill.

When I was very young, aside from my parents and some of their siblings I knew little or nothing of my heritage. I knew some of the light, happy moments of my mother's life, and just a little of the trauma of my father's early existence, and the surprising romance of their courtship (surprising to me because I had never envisioned them in that light), but knew little of them or their clan from before that. I remember just the shadows of my grandparents, but nothing of their past—of how they got to America, or of the families they left behind, or of the shtetls (villages) from which they escaped.

I suspect that such ignorance of family history is commonplace and it was because I wanted my children and their children to know more about from whom and what they came that I recorded their biographies and anecdotes. But while those printed recollections was meant as a gift to my kids, the time and thought that went into its production and the memories it invoked made it much more a gift to myself. Which is why I now recommend such an effort as a project for other seniors whose days are less than full. It would be good for their kids, but could be a sanity-saver for themselves.

And that is one of the values of such writing tasks for seniors with large inventories of past experiences: we can better use those memories to build the future and enhance the present.

Irrational Optimism

At 85, all the literature says I should be approaching old age. I'm reasonably sure that some day I'll get there, maybe even die at the end of the process, but I can understand that only in the abstract—I don't really believe it will happen to me. I have never accepted that any of those unpleasant or inconvenient rules of mortality applied to me and deep down I still don't—but I am getting closer.

For the first time in my life I now occasionally tie the fact of my age to the reality of life, recognizing the relationship between the accumulation of years and the end of their use. One of my new routines is reading the local obituaries—searching, of course, for the names of friends I hadn't seen for a while and may never see again. I am increasingly aware of limitations and the possibility that some old friend has died—a powerful reminder, not just of mortality, but more significantly of *my* mortality. I can accept the fact that it happens and can even come to terms with the logic and inevitability of death, just that I seem to have trouble moving it from my peripheral vision to a spot more centrally focused. It happened to my parents, but they were old—well, my dad was 74. And my sister died at 80—but she had been sick, so that's different. And various friends of mine died at ages ranging from about ten to seventy-five, but that's sort of a part of life and it's common knowledge that life is full of sad and senseless tragedies.

But clearly, none of that applies to me. After eight decades of denying both the fact and signs of aging, I have perfected the art of self-denial. I realize that for many, a long, serious illness can leave you lying somewhere between going and gone, but otherwise you can always exult in still having things to do. And that is a large part of how to approach that last phase—just keep planning and trying and doing. The beauty of life at any age, but a requisite for old age, is *Tomorrow*. As an 82-year-old billionaire, T. Boone Pickens spent his days promoting the long-term goal of harnessing the power of the wind, while fellow billionaire 94-year old Kirk Kerkorian was still maneuvering to buy General Motors—until the economy ruled otherwise. But regardless of need or skill or size of the prize, it is still the lures of Tomorrow that keep us in the race.

It is foolish, of course, to plan on immortality, but even more foolish—dangerously and destructively foolish—is to allot the limited time of that most important segment of your life (as each segment always is) to a downside. It is also true, of course, that we do not have as much control of our emotions or our physical condition or our psychological attitudes as this piece of literary buoyancy suggests, but we can try—we must try. The end may be tomorrow, but today I'm trying to finish this article, and tomorrow I'll adjust my backswing so I can break a hundred, and then I've got a very serious poker game with my friends, and I've got an appointment with Apple to learn how to better manipulate my new computer. This is not all just "make-work." Each activity means a lot to me, and even if I fail at several of these tasks, even if I still can't break a hundred and I lose my shirt (again) in the poker game and I never figure out that damn internet connection—so what? I assume I shall and I intend to use all my time and limited skills to those ends.

And that's the whole point. I'm doing all of this for me, and if I succeed in any or all of this I shall be way ahead of the game and happy and satisfied and busy planning the next tomorrow. And if it does not work as planned—again so what? We cannot plan all that effectively in the dark of the future, so even if my plans go awry I shall have had a lot more pleasure and fulfillment than could have been achieved with worry and anguish and remorse. In short, it is all mine to build and use and enjoy and it is the here and the now for me to embrace or reject—and if and how I screw it up affects nobody but me.

Of course, much of that last section is not altogether accurate. In one sense I am doing all of that for me, but in the larger sense it is for my wife and children so they will have much easier days while I am still around, and for my grandchildren so they will have some more good memories to help sustain them in *their* old age. And maybe I am even doing some of this in the name of vanity, flirting with the highly unlikely possibility that some small part of my last few efforts will outlive me and maybe contribute something to the world or society—or at least to somebody—and thereby help satisfy my ego. Hey, when you're old enough you're allowed to dream.

A Matter Of Principles

One of the intellectual benefits of aging is the ability to draw on experiences that had gone well or badly during our periods of growth, then to interpret our conclusions as universal truths. Such contrived insights are not a natural by-product of memories recorded and reexamined, but can effectively serve as a valuable guide for the future. And if judgments gained from those unsealed memories pass as wisdom, that may not be too far off the mark.

During the height of the Cold War, for example, the late Senator Joe McCarthy, whose reign was an embarrassment to our constitution, to our traditions and to the high moral code we like to believe is inherently ours, had become the icon of irresponsible representation. His politically inspired charges of conspiracy, treachery and disloyalty destroyed reputations, careers and lives and went uncurbed for several years, not effectively challenged until lawyer Joseph Welch, during hearings conducted by the army to investigate some of his more outrageous charges, asked, "At long last, sir, have you no sense of decency." Joe McCarthy was a bad man, "a sleazy bully" in the words of famed columnist Richard Rovere, obsessed with power, disinterested in truth and dangerously destructive to our nation. But as a threat he was hardly unique to our system. Nor will he be the last.

Of serious concern is that so few of our legislators seem to have learned from that experience—or have failed to properly monitor the performance of its members. We shall always have our fools and ideologues in positions of power, but our system of laws and logic, of checks and balances, is designed to guard against the abuses of legislative power, to protect the weakest from the more powerful and the most powerful from the mob. If the elected guardians of our democracy, for reasons of greed or power or cowardice, fail in that task, that is the more troubling threat. It was Joe McCarthy's colleagues who failed in their obligation to uphold the spirit and intent and integrity of our democratic system who let us down— even more than the culprit himself.

And that is one of the disconcerting problems of aging—we may have learned from the past, but are unable to extend its lessons to our leaders. It is now a half-century later and those same legislators, under different names and following different drummers, are still pursuing votes and self-interests at the expense of national honor or personal integrity, still subverting the principles of the Constitution in favor of Party loyalty and reelection.

Effective legislative voices from both the Left and the Right are necessary to maintain a workable balance in our system, but this requires manipulating the levers of power honestly and honorably. We need our system of competing political parties—of liberal and conservative voices—to effectively debate the issues. We need spokespeople representing conflicting views to deal with the present and shape the future, but those voices, above all else, must be *principled*.

Adherence to established principles, pursued with integrity, free of obligation to Party or patron, must be the standard for the gift of our vote. Anything less is a perversion of our system. The billions being spent by drug companies and financial institutions and military supply contractors to bribe (see: "lobby") our legislators, however well clothed in clichés of nobility or manipulated by tortured logic, seriously weakens the health of our nation.

And that is one of the lessons of aging. Those insights we had gained along the way is not evidence of wisdom, but some of those bits of information that we may have absorbed could prove invaluable in effectively resolving our nation's affairs. By now we should have a reasonably clear view of our political and cultural environment and should use that knowledge to protect our society. As seniors we may have seen this pattern of consuming self-interest before, but we like to believe it belongs to a different culture, perhaps to those smaller nations in today's headlines that are controlled by autocrats with no sense of responsibility for those they rule. But as seniors we have also seen enough changes during our lifetimes to give us pause in our inherent confidence in the inviolable virtue in our own system.

In our earliest days there was a perhaps naive confidence in the power of principles to guide our legislative decisions, of a reliance on the ethical implications of our Constitution. That earlier assumption, whether or not deserved, is no longer applicable. A representative of the people who is torn between his duty to his nation or the lure of his political ambitions or the material rewards of compliance—and who succumbs to those temptations—is dishonest with his constituency and a danger to his nation.

And for those insights we really don't need the wisdom of the ages or their aged advocates. We simply must select our goals reasonably and fairly, then pursue them with honor and principle—remembering that it is our grandchildren who will inherit the fruit or the folly of our actions.

Eight Decades Later

It was Aesop, the ancient Teller of Tales, who first identified the Seven Stages of Man as childhood through old age, further noting that each stage is enlivened by anticipation of what comes next. That makes sense for the first Six Stages, but for the Seventh Stage—that of "old age" —a problem emerges: there is no "next."

Seniors, having moved beyond the growing pains and pleasures of their early and middle years, are increasingly in need of new challenges to keep their interest alive. Watching the children and grandchildren mature can be immensely satisfying, but participation in the process is limited. For more advanced seniors something more is needed, some new sources of challenge or stimulation to sustain an interest in life. Maybe even a few small personal victories of little consequence to help energize our fading egos. Without the tests and trials implied in Aesop's "anticipation of what comes next" too many of us will be left with increasingly bland days, empty of suspense or surprise or success, so it is essential that alternative interests and activities be found.

Fortunately, the range of new fields of interest available for examination is broad and plentiful. The application of new routines for those of us occupying space between late middle-aged and old, between retired and superfluous, exempts us from many of the responsibilities of the workplace and of parenthood, leaving us free to experiment with new pursuits and to embrace them with some degree of anticipation and enthusiasm—or even to reject them without guilt or regret. The problem is that too often, somewhere between free and overwhelmed is "bored" and that is no way to deal with the Seventh Stage of life.

For many seniors transitioning from occupied to disengaged, a challenge of almost any sort can be a very welcome source of renewed energy and satisfaction. It is the challenge, the simple fact of competition and not the win or loss, that brings to the surface the pleasure that had defined "success" in our earlier lives. And there is no single classification of competition that serves better than others, simply whatever stimulates our drive or gratifies our ego. In short, whatever turns us on. And that list can be as arbitrary as it is extensive, including all the games in the inventory of our culture— poker or tennis or chess—even actively taking sides in the game of politics. There is a satisfaction in filling all the squares in Sudoku and in completing all the words in the crossword puzzle and unmatched is the pleasure in beating your opponent in golf—closely followed by improving your own game since last you played. But even when losing in any of these contests, simply having tried hard and done reasonably well provides a certain sense of satisfaction.

And however difficult it might be to adjust our behavior to conform with the requirements of maturity—such as my giving in to the demands of my kids to wear a helmet when riding my bicycle— at least the veneer of responsibility can be worth the sacrifice.

None of us is without some dream or distant goal, however insignificant its substance or unlikely its achievement or illogical its pursuit. No matter how much we have or how little we need we all want for something. And no matter how trivial or unlikely its realization, it is the pursuit itself that keeps us on the trail of tomorrow. It was the collapse of the economy, for example, not the limitations of age that moved 94-year-old billionaire Kirk Kerkorian to finally gave up trying to buy General Motors (presumably as protection for his old age).

And that's the point. Even the most irrational goals of the dreamy-eyed ancients among us have a role to play—because without those goals we exist as little more than fillers of space. Whatever shape it takes, "tomorrow" remains the hope for us all, regardless of need or skill or size of the prize. Because the alternative to planning our future is simply to quit—and whatever your age or condition, such surrender is unacceptable and from it there is no return.

I suspect most of us had doubts while growing up—struggling against the competition to get a date for the movies or the prom, or later to make the team, or still later to find our place in the firm. For a while we were heroes to our kids who thought we were really smart, or that our athletic skills were very nearly unmatched, or that we understood the deeper, darker mysteries of the unknown. Unfortunately, that faded when the kids grew older and wiser and began to beat us at our own games. Now my routine is to seek out one of my grandchildren for help with my computer or to retrieve missed messages on my cell phone.

But all of that is all right, because it means I am still involved and at our age that is all that really counts. It may too late to make our place in the world, but enjoying the place we had made earlier is a very pleasurable and satisfying alternative.

Measuring Up

N obody said it was easy. Running a household efficiently and effectively, keeping within budget and pleasing all its residents, is an intimidating challenge for even the most efficient and dedicated of managers.

And running a business that satisfies the needs of the market it serves, meanwhile remaining profitable for its investors, is a task that makes household responsibilities seem like a walk in the park.

But running a country that is attentive to the many needs of its diverse population and to all the varied interests that are necessary and responsible for reaching those goals—accounting for the dreams and traditions that have guided us and sustained us since our founding more than two centuries ago—makes all the rest little more than child's play.

All of which means that our nation's representatives in both houses of Congress, making decisions about how to plan our future and run our country, must rely on much more than the technical skills of their advisors—or on their own political dreams—or the personal goals of their deep-pocketed supporters. They must have a set of core principles by which to set their standards of performance and by which to measure the results.

Running an organization the size and complexity of the United States is truly mind-boggling. Even aside from organizing the programs and personnel necessary to keep us afloat and preparing for such unforeseeable disasters as wars and hurricanes and plagues, just the task of keeping incomes and expenses in some sort of balance is enough to traumatize the most insensitive soul. So it may be a bit unfair to come down too hard on those who run the show from Washington, but they are the ones, after all, who insist on the credit when things go well and who point disapproving fingers at their critics when it falls apart, so they are also the ones who must ultimately be held accountable. And the essence of that responsibility is the welfare of the people by whom this nation was built and for whom these legislators serve. Now their most difficult and delicate problem is in defining the needs of our nation—honestly and honorably—and determining how those needs can best be met.

Aye, and therein lies the quandary. There are those who feel that Big Business provides the jobs that fuel the economy that feeds the people that builds the future that keeps us happy, so it is the needs of Big Business that must be attended and nurtured and protected. Others narrow the list to just those most consequential players like the biggest banks and global investment firms and major defense contractors and others who are charged with keeping us free in a hostile world . . . and fuels the economy that feeds the people that builds the . . . etc. And still others concentrate their support on the many temples of worship designed to sustain us when all else fails to satisfactorily fuel the economy that feeds the people that builds . . . etc.

Or maybe, and more likely, none of the above—or at least, none of the above should be granted the honored spot on center stage. The original focus of our founding was on the people to be served. Instituting the most efficient means for the provision of that service, of course, is an essential part of the process, but that remains secondary to the basic goal of providing for the people. In the Constitution's pledge to "promote the general Welfare" it is the People who are the focus of those must be served—at least on a par with the providers of that service. Efficiency in the provision and distribution of those services is essential, of course, but there must be a core set of principles by which those needs are identified and on which their programs of support are designed and built.

Helping secure the health and satisfy the needs of profit-oriented suppliers in order to protect their firms and employees and customers is a reasonable responsibility of government, but extending those benefits to the rest of our nation's citizens—even without ties to business—is no less a national obligation.

It may not be fair to concentrate too rigorously on the occasional misdeed or mismanagement or mistake that marks so much of our nation's performance when so many options are in play, but ultimately our actions must be guided by concern for the well-being of our larger population.

And I suggest that the basic principles most compatible with our people and our traditions are those articulated in our Constitution. In that sacred document's pledge to "form a more perfect Union" is the presumed promise to provide the most efficient, reliable, honorable standard on which to build and protect our future—and that overrides all competing goals and interests.

Off The Path

Personal experience is the most reliable source of information for understanding and resolving some of the complexities of life and as seniors we have an enviably wide range of memories from which to draw. For those issues that predate us, however, our own experiences may not be enough. We have to go back to an earlier period, perhaps back to the beginning. But for that, of course, we have to agree on when the beginning began.

For some humanists it was about the time that Adam lost his rib and his heart to Eve. Many scientists, however, opt for the moment of The Big Bang 15 billion years ago, while a few originalists hold to their own more unique fantasies, such as Bishop Ussher who insisted the world's first day began on a morning in 4004 BC.

For issues affecting a somewhat more contemporary world, however, there are more relevant starting points a bit less remote. Most Americans, for example, think of the beginning in terms of the birth of our nation in 1776, when a group of patriots said "enough" to foreign control and struck out on their own, declaring that "all men are created equal . . . with . . . unalienable Rights," later adding the promise to "establish Justice . . . promote the general Welfare, and secure the Blessings of Liberty to ourselves and our posterity." That was the start of a whole new era, unique in the history of Man, in which the citizens of a nation became the focus and the purpose of its government.

Not even the most antique among our seniors can remember the launching of that moment, but they may connect with the spirit and humanitarian goals that are the rich legacy of that new beginning. We like to look back over our past and credit our development on the skills we acquired and the lessons we learned, but of special significance are some of our more distant roots—those humanitarian principles ingrained in our Constitution. They were a major factor in the growth of our nation and helped shape the character of our predecessors—and continue to play a role in who we are today. But that noble profile is becoming ever more foreign in what seems to be our future.

We are still a humanitarian and generous people, but in recent decades our pride as a nation sworn to "establish Justice . . . [and] . . . promote the general Welfare" has been slowly redirecting its attention to programs centered on avoidance of taxes. It is natural, of course, that our primary concern be our families and ourselves, but we have always been more than that. Our traditions have always kept us focused on principles and on the basic needs of our neighbors, but that original concentration on the "welfare of our people" is beginning to drift into a future increasingly less inviting.

Now we as seniors have a special role to play. We are not smarter than our younger compatriots, nor are we more sensitive to the moral requirements of a good life, but because we are a bit closer to the end of our adventure we have a little less to lose in objectivity. And perhaps with that objectivity we can better appreciate the value of the principles that marked our nation's past and that now seems to be in remission or retreat. It is our obligation, then, to take the lead in elevating those principles to a more central position in our society.

Simply avoiding inconvenience is not who we are. Going into World War II we were still suffering from the most devastating economic disaster in our history, but working together—freezing wages in the defense industry and raising income taxes on the highest earners to as much as 91 percent—we shared the burden, won the war, and set our nation on the path to one of the most stimulating, most satisfying—and most profitable—periods in our history.

And we seniors may remember, too, the satisfying sense of national unity that marked our efforts during that war as men rushed to join the military and women, glorified as Rosie the Riveter, joined the work force to build our planes and tanks. We shared the pain and we shared the sacrifice. We really were " . . . one nation . . . indivisible."

Now, as seniors in a new age, it is our turn to do what is necessary to bring back that sense of union. Saving our nation's honor requires refocusing on our principles and more equitably sharing the burdens of citizenship. And as a nation of idealism, conceived and fashioned in a spirit of purity of purpose, that is fully in keeping with our traditions.

And even if that reverie is no more solid than a child's dream or a fading senior's fantasy, we are still that much further ahead simply for having set goals a bit higher than "tax reduction" or other mechanics of governance. And is a whole lot closer to who we really are—as a nation and as a people.

Behind The Mask

For a while in my forties I sported a great bushy black beard, a thick mustache and got a crew cut. I don't know that it did much for my appearance, but I enjoyed an unreasonable degree of comfort in the anonymity it seemed to provide, experiencing a certain sense of security in being able to thus hide my face and feeling behind my mask. (An unexpected but very gratifying benefit was the simplicity and speed of my morning routine—no shaving and no combing.) I have since come to the conclusion that the mask of age serves much the same purpose.

One of the truths of old age, although less clear to those still struggling to reach it, is that except for having been around longer, the old are really very little different from what they were when they were young—essentially the same saps or savants and as foolish or profound as in their earlier years. They are the same people, simply with more experience under their belts. How they use that experience is a reflection more of their essence than of their longevity. While the wrinkled skin adds a sense of mystery to the moment, the reality is that with the accumulation of decades the antique survivors are given credit for wisdom and insights that may never have really been a part of their inventory.

As an example of my own senior standing, for instance, I often find myself categorized by my juniors as somewhere between a sage (nice, but unlikely) and something approaching a doddering old fool (I do not dodder). The fact, however, is simply that I am still me—the same me as before, but older. That does not mean we don't change with age, simply that it is not necessarily for the better, nor that we have become more wise. Merely that we have lived through more experiences and may, as a consequence, have learned a bit more (*may* have learned more—but not necessarily). A part of the problem is the natural deterioration that plagues the human animal. The world is changing and our perception of the world is changing even faster, but as we age fewer of us are able or willing to deal with those changes. Too many of us have lost our passion—we have simply stopped trying. We have given in to the debilitating platitudes that are used to define old age and have accepted that status. It's easier than fighting.

And that, in turn, may account for some of the increasing conservatism of older people. I had often wondered why the old tended to be so much more conservative than the young, why young firebrands changed direction with age. Having long identified myself as a Liberal, I would hate to think the wisdom I had acquired over decades of trial, error and observation were no more significant than the coarsening of my skin and the graying or losing of my hair. I suspect instead that conservatism, as the counterpoint to liberalism, wins out simply because it requires less thought, less challenge, less activity.

This is not to denigrate the role of conservatism, but recognizes its purpose as a protector of values or procedures that have proven valid and successful in the past. Conserving the best parts of our heritage is as valuable to our future as finding new ways to achieve old, but neglected goals. And for old people who have lost their taste for fight, that can be a very appealing alternative to seeking radical new paths. It may be that we are fearful that if things go wrong we shall not have the time or strength to set them straight. Challenge, after all, can be work, often fueled by an energy increasingly scarce in most older citizens. It may generate new ideas not yet fully developed and that implies a responsibility that many seniors are no longer able to accept. Such change requires planning and arguing and convincing—and then it may all go nowhere or, if implemented, blow up in our face. Conservatism, on the other hand, requires standing guard. They are both vital to the success of our democracy, but liberalism tends to be more a young person's game, drawing on the idealism and energies more likely to fade with age.

But where we stand on the political platform is not really the critical factor. More beneficial to our heirs than the names of the victors or the identity of their party are the lessons we absorb and then impart to the emerging generations. The key, after all, is not so much the conclusion of each dispute, but the principles and the level of integrity guiding the process. Unfortunately, the current legislative political posturing in exchange for funds or votes is antithetical to our traditions and dangerous to our future—a concern as obvious to the young as it is to the "wise old codgers."

No, age does not make us wise—it merely makes us old. But with those years—if we are lucky—it also makes us experienced and with that experience we are better able to draw conclusions not immediately obvious to the young. It may take all of our declining passions to take strong stands about our society, but I suspect those passions are more likely to strengthen us—both ourselves and our nation—than to drain us.

And it is certainly a whole lot better than giving up or giving in.

Old Age: The Start Of Something New

Most seniors have learned a lot in the seven or eight decades they had spent building their futures, but some of those lessons no longer apply. It used to be that one good way of relieving our financial burdens, for example, was to work longer hours or change jobs, but that doesn't work too well for those of us in our eighties. Even buying cheap start-up stock in some future "Yahoo" or "Google" is appealing, but being unable to reap the rewards of those investments for the years or decade it will take those companies to grow does tend to throw a damper on the project. And for antique couch potatoes anxious to get back into shape, running marathons or entering mountain-bike races may have some serious downsides.

Programs and techniques designed to build a better future for our younger selves generally have limited application as we grow old, so we should concentrate more on those routes and routines that have a connection with who we are today rather than on that character in our memory. And even if those reduced and redesigned efforts are unattainable and we fall short of our substitute goals, failing to meet our own easier standards—so what? The reward, after all, is in the satisfaction of the pursuit rather than in the prize.

Meanwhile, one of the lessons from those years of growth that still has application is that we must not quit. In our reduced physical state we may have to limit our aspirations or perhaps change our definition of success, but if the alternative is a vacuum late in our lives, we have no choice—we must keep on doing and keep on trying. New interests or skills for old seniors may seem a fruitless pursuit, but simply the search for new horizons, with or without success, can be invigorating and in itself worth the effort. Struggling to learn a new language, for example, may leave us tongue-tied or mute, or the tables we built in our new woodwork shop may never be stable enough to balance our after-dinner drink, but that should not negate the value of the effort. More than the achievement, after all, is the pleasure of the pursuit, the satisfaction of the drive itself. At this point in our lives, it is the thrill of the search and the gratification of having tried that continues to keep us afloat.

The fact is that the older we get the fewer options we have. Many favored activities are now beyond our skills or strength, and lurking in the wings are those age-related problems of ill health, so new paths to a productive future—a necessary component of a satisfying old age—must be developed.

When Diane Keaton won the Academy Award for "Annie Hall" she was congratulated by Audrey Hepburn, a female icon she had long idolized. Ms. Hepburn told the new winner that the future would be hers, a prediction designed to thrill the soul. But rather than exultation Ms. Keaton remembers being fearful of a fading future, for both herself and Ms. Hepburn. She was convinced that past accolades remain mired in the past and that after a period of celebration, even the more impressive achievements have a limited shelf life and must be reinvigorated or replaced. In affect, thank goodness for yesterday, but what about tomorrow?

In addition to luck, finding a satisfying and productive path to a senior's future requires patience, a lot of work—and an active imagination. Even the most outlandish, illogical efforts can occasionally produce astonishing results. One of the better recent examples of the value of persistence in the face of hopelessness is the drive of James Arrundra Henry. "Jim" Henry had been a lobster fisherman all his life, from his very early childhood until recently when it finally became clear that he was just too old to continue. When he was in his nineties he moved into a Senior Home in Connecticut. It's enough. Time to quit. But he didn't quit. Having spent his entire childhood at sea, the last 47 years as a fishing boat captain. Totally illiterate, never having learned to read, he could not even sign his name.

Time for a change. At age 96 and with the help and encouragement of fellow senior residents, he learned the alphabet, learned to sign his name, then at age 97 began to write a book about his life's experiences. And at age 98 he completed and published that book, "In A Fisherman's Life"—all of its 29 chapters. And his reaction? "I'm in a cloud—I can't believe—almost impossible to believe—I'm the happiest man in the world."

And that is the point of these few words. There is much about which to be troubled by the unpleasant realities of aging, but also available are the fantasies that flow from the blind, perhaps even irrational, hopes for the future. The remaining days may be short, but they need not be altogether dispiriting. The fact remains that an active search for even a small piece of tomorrow is the best route for saving a big part of today.

The Business Of Government

It was President Calvin Coolidge in the early 1920s who asserted that "the business of America is business." If they had television in those days he would have been the target of all the late-night TV comedians, but we now discover that he was not necessarily foolish or glib—just prescient.

The concept of running the government as a business has much to recommend it. Political conservatives, as custodians of our democracy's traditions and with responsibility for maintaining the stability of our nation's economic well-being, pride themselves on serving as "the party of Business," embracing the politics of efficiency, security and profit. Innovation, they claim, has its place, but the evidence of proven performance transcends the uncertainty of gambling on attractive, but unproven ideas. As a successful business, after all, our country could assure stability and make funds available for the necessities of a good, or at least adequate, life for all its citizens. With such a no-nonsense, conservative approach to our nation's governance, it could be claimed that the important needs of the People—health care, education, food, housing—will be adequately attended. Successful businesses are built on knowing the needs of their customers and employing the most efficient ways by which to satisfy those needs.

At least that's the theory. Unfortunately, the problem with the government's current business model is that a large part of its original customer base—the working middle-class who comprise the vast majority of our population—has been downgraded to the status more of inventory than of client. It is now the suppliers rather than those most in need who are the primary recipients of our government's attention. And now that segment of our population most dangerously impacted by our tottering economy because they have no reserves and no alternatives, are further threatened by fiscal policies focusing on the reduction of aid to the indigent as the best way by which to balance our budget.

The conservative philosophy of keeping larger business firms healthy in order to provide jobs in the future is reasonable and potentially productive—within principled limits. Adjusting those limits to the politics of the moment, however, can be dangerous. An offensive example of surpassing reasonable limits, for instance, was the legislative favor to the coal mining industry to help them cut their costs by reducing the safety rules then in place. Unfortunately, in 2006 the inaction of the regulators charged with oversight and enforcement of even those new relaxed rules led to the West Virginia Sago coal mine disaster—and its loss of twelve miners' lives.

Manipulating the system to make friends and win votes often works, but is not the best way to serve the people or the Democratic process. Our Constitution, the founding document setting the tone and defining the goals of our democracy, insists that its primary mission is to "promote the general Welfare" of our citizens, thereby "form[ing] a more perfect Union." That goal remains unchanged for conservative and liberal leaders alike, but the loss of the higher principles of governance makes it a very costly and dangerous tactic.

The credible conservative philosophy that by making businesses profitable, working people will find the employment they need to provide adequate resources for a better life is reasonable—when approached with integrity. Buying political support by reducing taxes for the affluent, however, or helping industry by not enforcing such environmental safeguards as the clean-air or clean-water regulations, is dangerous and dishonorable—a form of "trickle-down relief". An alternative approach would be to start the process by identifying the unmet needs of our people, analyze ways to provide the assistance needed to bring them up to speed and *then* determine the best and most efficient tactics to meet those ends.

In his second Inaugural Address in 1937, Franklin Roosevelt, noting the shame of "one-third of a nation, ill-housed, ill-clad, ill-nourished" said, "The government is competent when *all* who compose it work as trustees *for the whole people.*" The Founders' pledge to "promote the General welfare" is one of the bedrock principles of our nation—the essence of who we are. Rather than trying to create an environment conducive to fuller employment so people will *eventually* find work—also known as "trickle down"—it should be mandatory that everyone have their essential needs fulfilled and *then* find the best way to manage the process. In the present scheme of things we too easily lose our focus, concentrating on the well-being of our suppliers rather than of our people, which puts the citizens several rungs lower than that of business. It is reasonable to support businesses in order to help the poor, but the ground rules must be set by the needs of the people—their customers—rather than by the demands of their stockholders.

To some degree, President Coolidge was right—business does have a major role in the business of our country, but instead of concentrating solely on methods of easing quality controls or bypassing environmental standards to meet that burden, our concern must include addressing the needs of the people to be served. Very simply, in both the planning and the process, the *people* must be our focus.

On Our Own Time

It was some years ago that I was first introduced to the highly touted joys of retirement—and I was hooked. Waking at seven in the morning, hearing the birds celebrating their small victories over slow-moving worms, then rolling over in bed without any attendant feelings of guilt—what's not to like?

It was the promise of a great new time of life—feared by some, overly glorified by others, and badly played by many. Letting the birds and worms fight it out is an interesting sideshow, but it is a battle that does not add much to our day. Now that we've been freed of meeting schedules set by the obligations of jobs we no longer have, we can deal with routines of our own choosing.

The freedom of retirement can be a wonderful gift, but it can also be a challenge. Doing nothing can be very appealing, but it wears thin very quickly and can be dangerously self-destructive. Much of our careers in the workplace were directed toward providing for our families and our futures, but now that the goals have been met or are no longer relevant, that same need for productivity remains. Just that the rewards have changed—the productivity flows in different directions.

For myself, I can now focus on those pursuits for which I never before had sufficient time, such as building wobbly tables to support equipment I rarely use, or giving full attention to improving a golf game which inexplicably seems to deteriorate with practice. Now

I'm busy writing letters of protest or praise to people and companies who rarely answer, or little notes of clarification to people who took offense at my last notes, or struggling to understand the mysteries of my computer in order to write those notes and apologies.

Leading a life of indolence doesn't take a lot of training and can be addictive, so background experience is helpful. While my years in the fabric business, for example, taught me no retirement skills except, perhaps, woolgathering (sorry 'bout that) and my travel agency added little more, the disciplines they encouraged are good for any age and activity—or inactivity, if that better represents my chosen path.

The point is that movement itself is important—not necessarily the direction of that movement. My half-century of skiing, for example, need not be off the agenda, but now clearly off the table—or off the slopes—is taking hills too steep or moguls too high. Nor will I stay on the mountain until the last chairlift closes. But it makes little difference how much my athletic skills and routines have diminished—I've given up trying to show off. My kids have long known my limitations and finally I, too, have admitted to them, so now it's just for the fun of it—and that is all I now need.

Not that I was ever resentful of my full-time-and-a-half work routine, but there's no question that holding a job, supporting a family and raising children really does cut into a person's free time. I had always managed to find time for satisfying activities unrelated to my job—perhaps playing squash with my friend at mid-afternoon of a business-day, or taking a couple of days off to see a show in New York with my wife. But now with the freedom of retirement I can participate openly rather than surreptitiously—and without feelings of guilt.

Nevertheless, retired time is not totally free time, not completely without some degree of guilt attached to inactivity. Several decades ago, for example, my wife's father, an untrained and unrecognized scholar who used to complain that he was two hundred years behind in his reading, also retired. But even then he had to deal with a new and unexpected obstacle, complaining that "you can't read Dostoevsky in the morning."

The character and nature of old age obligations are different from those of our younger years. Our kids need us less and our mortgage has been paid, but we still have a place in the world, we still have people around us—whether strangers or family—who need our help or advice. If it is true that you can't read Dostoevsky in the morning, it is also true that life, even during its golden phase, cannot be devoted exclusively to the joys of self-indulgence. Among other reasons, it is because indulgence is that much sweeter when it stands in sharp relief to the pursuit of some more productive effort or obligation.

And we've got plenty of gratifying alternative obligations right here in River City. Many local organizations exist that have undertaken to assist citizens who cannot assist themselves—to feed the poor, care for the helpless, tend the ill, shelter the homeless, teach the young. They are all seriously underfunded and depend for their very existence on volunteers who have the time to give. An almost uniform reaction of those involved with such organizations and services is the rare and remarkable fact that *everybody* benefits—the organizations that continue functioning even while inadequately funded; those recipients whose troubled lives are made bearable by the services provided; and the volunteers whose service to their fellows adds meaning to their own lives.

In short, we don't have to quit when we quit—there's always more to do. After all those years of earning a living this might seem like working another job, but now we can do it on our own time and at our own pace—and to the fulfillment of our own most personal needs.

Doing For Others: A Blessing For Both

It has been just weeks since the casual pace of my life was replaced by the drama of an unanticipated medical problem—one that disrupted my routine, threatened my survival, and left me forever indebted to the skills of a University of Michigan surgical team. Later, preparing to leave the hospital for my return to civilian life, I was encouraged by many to use that experience as a subject for a future column. A great idea—except that there was more to the memory than the sutures.

But the fuller story begins a couple of years earlier.

Several years ago, my niece, Katy, graduated from college; joined a few friends in buying and refurbishing an old, discarded school bus; installed a toilet and stove; and set out on her big adventure. After several months on the road her natural sense of social responsibility began to replace her limited focus on fun—so she joined the Peace Corps.

Her base was a settlement in Zambia where her assignment was to oversee and assist the lost children of the village, most of whom had been orphaned by HIV/Aids. The story is much too long to detail as a sidebar in this short article, but the essence is that because of her dedication, her very lively imagination and a lot of very hard work she was able to solicit enough funds and enlist enough local support to build a new school. Then, through a combination of guile and bribery (the kids could use the school's highly coveted athletic facilities only if they attended classes and some lectures on the cause and prevention of HIV/Aids), she managed to educate some, save others from deadly infection and finally to offer them a life better than that of their parents.

The Peace Corps was born in Ann Arbor, so I knew all the necessary facts of its purpose and growth, but I had never really thought much about its breadth or spirit before. For the first time I began to have a better understanding of the extent of the benefits it might provide to those it was designed to help, and of the role it might play in the growth and lives of its volunteers. For Katy it was the beginning of a life dedicated to serving the needs of Man. And for me it was a template to help me better understand and appreciate the humanitarian instincts of so many of our people.

So much for the prelude.

In preparation for my surgery I was introduced to a nurse who was part of the surgeon's team. She mentioned in passing that she had just returned from Kenya, a country I had visited for a safari several years earlier. When I indicated how much I had enjoyed my visit to that region she almost exploded with enthusiasm. She told me that she had spent several months there, working very nearly around the clock as a volunteer medical aide for that most needy population. The work was hard, the hours endless, the conditions horrible—and she loved it. She said that never in her life had she felt more productive and rewarded and is now committed to going back to do more of the same.

After the operation I was attended by a number of post-op nurses, all of whom were smart, pleasant, sensitive and deeply concerned about my pain and my future. The other issue that united many of them was their shared desire to help the ill and indigent in foreign countries that had no access to medical assistance and no funds to obtain it and were therefor doomed to early and often horrible deaths. They all revealed to me their very strong desire to once again contribute their services to future medical relief programs for those doomed third-world citizens.

After my discharge that pattern of humanitarian concern was again reflected in comments from the several aides that came to my home to remove stitches or oversee other details of my rehabilitation progress. One nurse's aide, for example, whose husband and three young children made a month of service in distant third world countries an impossible task, insists that the family spend at least one vacation week each year providing assistance where most needed in this country. Her goal, beyond providing relief for those served, is to help instill a sense of humanitarian responsibilities in her children.

If my exiting the hospital and recuperation period alive can be rated as interesting and if recounting the amazing skills of those professionals who got me to that point shares that honor, then my time in the hospital may be worth an article. But of much greater interest (except to my family) is a national characteristic generally overlooked by the daily headlines and network news. Necessarily missing from such reviews are the remarkable contributions of so many of our neighbors who care and perform, all in the interest of unselfish humanitarian service—and all without acclamation or even notice. Our attention, of course, will always be attracted to issues of national consequence or the drama of political bickering by legislators fighting for reelection, but very many of our people— many who are the core and the character of our nation—are much more than that. Their efforts will, of course, remain obscured by the daily trauma affecting our larger population, but their contributions to the needy of the world remain fruitful and inspiring—and are amazingly more common than is generally recognized.

And maybe that was the lesson of my hospital stay.

End Of The World

Harold Camping, a radio evangelist with a massive following, firmly believes that the world is coming to an end—and soon. The idea is not new to him. His first "last day" was for mid-September, 1995, then later revised to March 31, 1995, then most recently for May 21, 2011. But he does have stamina, so maybe now he is starting to get the hang of it.

And before him there was the most prominent doomsday prophesier, William Miller, who foresaw the world ending on March 31, 1843—or maybe 1844, he wasn't sure.

And before them were the Maya, whose Dresden Codex made a similar prediction in the 11th or 12th century.

The "end of the world" has come and gone many times during the past centuries and we seem not to be too much the worse for wear. Of course, that doesn't mean that it won't happen, and its ultimate success could be a terrible inconvenience, but even then we should not just quit. In one way or another it happens all the time—reappearing each time in a different guise reflecting a different aspect of a broad range of widely different trauma. But as with many such ordeals, the level of shock it generates depends on the welcome—or rejection—it receives from its victims.

I think of my father, for example, whose remarkably hard and thankless childhood marked him as a perfect candidate for the end of the world. His barren, loveless early years as a stepchild rejected by his stepfather and cruelly targeted by his stepbrothers was a plot straight out of Dickens. Until, that is, he married the girl of his dreams—my mother. Together the two of them opened a small business, had three children, and for the first time enabled him to enjoy some degree of social success and independence and pride. Then the Depression hit. He lost it all—his house, his business, his pride—all of the ego-energizing evidence of his success. He was distraught. He was left with nothing—except my mother, the eternal, irrational optimist. Somehow with her confidence, her skills, her hard work and her husband they were able to get a few bucks together and try again. It worked and they survived happily and productively for many decades more.

More stunning and inspiring was the experience and reaction of British theoretical physicist and cosmologist, Stephen Hawking. At age 21, at the start of a promising career as a Professor of Mathematics, he came down with ALS (Lou Gehrig's Disease), a condition that destroys nerve cells in the brain and spinal cord, leaving its victim paralyzed in both voice and movement until permanently silenced by a much too early death. Now, Hawking, 48 years later, totally paralyzed, able to speak only through a computer voice simulator activated by twitching a cheek muscle, still writes, teaches, lectures, and is highly revered in the worlds of physics and cosmology.

And after all these years of immobility, without a voice to express his thoughts or arms to express his enthusiasm or even a wink to express his humor—although he does manage a small smile to express his pleasures—he still has thoughts of advice for those similarly afflicted, either by ALS or other such debilitating diseases: "My advice to other disabled people would be, concentrate on things your disability doesn't prevent you doing well, and don't regret the things it interferes with. Don't be disabled in spirit, as well as physically."

Predicting the future is even more difficult than understanding the present, so foreseeing the "end of the world" is not an easy task. After thirteen billion years, the world is still reeling from the effects of its Big Bang, so it is hardly surprising that it might finally be fading. But if the determination and perseverance of the many millions of blighted or bedeviled counterparts of my father throughout the world who still fight and occasionally emerge victorious, and if even those relatively few shining stars like Stephen Hawking, can overcome their indescribably debilitating handicaps to advance the scientific skills of the world to such astonishing new heights, then the end of the world can probably be kept at bay for at least a little longer.

The world seems to be going along pretty well at the moment, but it is still filled with its conflicts and controversies, with its treasures and tragedies—and its very uncertain future. Nevertheless, if the same fighting spirit shown by my parents is mirrored by even some small percentage of those many millions of oppressed people worldwide, then overcoming those pending tragedies—however limited—is a victory to be celebrated by us all. And if that determination holds as well for the Steve Hawkings that produce the intellectual needs of society well into their debilitating old age, that evidence of strength should keep our world going for more than a bit longer.

For seniors, the end of life is the end of the world, of their world, but even a modest postponement can be much more than a minor victory. Down the road, of course, we will all have to quit the race, but until then the magnitude of those small victories has a role in the way the world operates. In much the same way that my father fought to regain his losses and his pride, and that Stephen Hawking struggled—successfully—to continue his scientific advances, many seniors nearing the end of their existence can often, by fighting back, change the nature or timing of the process.

The future of the world is not truly dependent on the nature and outcome of these personal struggles, of course, but for many seniors nearing the end of their tenure, it is not overreaching to recall the words of America's resident philosopher, Yogi Bera, who famously insisted that "it ain't over 'til it's over."

A Changed World For Seniors

The world, it is a'changing. We all know that. We've seen it ourselves and we had it verified by the lectures of Bob Dylan, but the speed and magnitude of the change is more dramatic than we seniors had ever imagined. I was reminded of that still again when I put down my quill pen to send an e-mail notice to some friends that a meeting was to be held at my house a few weeks hence. One response, arriving at what seemed like moments later, was an apology for being unable to attend. He was out of town and wouldn't be back for a few days, adding, "It's Spring here in Beijing."

I know that for we octogenarians the marvels of the new world are far beyond our scientific backgrounds, technologically rooted as we are in the Middle-Ages. I know, too, that most seniors share my awe and utter confusion with those kids who spend all their days tweeting on twitter and connecting on Skype and participating in all those many other mysterious rituals of the Internet Age. And maybe that's why God invented grandchildren, who seem to have come into the world endowed with enough understanding of the intricacies of Twenty-First Century science to help their internet-illiterate grandparents.

But please do not misunderstand me. My frustration is troubling and very annoying, but it is not altogether a surrender. My inadequacies in the obscure details of the internet age slow me down and leave me increasingly dependent "on the kindness of strangers" (and caring grandchildren), but the upside of the new speed of life is that it allows us more time to search and savor the environment we still have.

For many seniors it is too late in the game to make their mark in big business or power politics or televised sports, so they assume the game is about over, that their moment in the sun has been blotted out by the gloom of their twilight. But lost opportunities of the past need not fashion their future. The grand goals of youth may have been inspirational decades earlier, but the glories of old age respond to much more modest achievements. Doing the best you can, even in a very limited sphere, can be pleasurable, reassuring and readily valuable.

For seniors struggling in the vacuum of days without purpose there are still challenges without end. If physical action is what turns us on, for example, we have golf courses beckoning us from all across the landscape, and all with the promise of scoring a ninety-eight after a lifetime of 105s. And as the seasons change and we object to looking for balls lost in piles of fresh snow, we can go indoors for tennis or squash or badminton.

Or we can go another route entirely and exercise our cerebral selves by more thoroughly learning the history of our nation, or by studying the ancient societies of Greece and Rome, or by reading antique scripts by long dead scholars—doing it on our own or with the aid of the vast inventory of classes and lectures available from the many experts in our midst.

But even more satisfying is the late-in-life potential of filling empty days with activities of significant social or humanitarian impact. All around us are groups devoted to the well-being of everything from lost animals to lost souls, providing us with unbounded opportunities to transform our spare and otherwise wasted hours into richly rewarding and productive lives of service. Readily available, too, are the many opportunities to volunteer in teaching the illiterate young to read, or giving tutorial aid to youngsters needing help to graduate high-school, or simply in finding a place in any one of the many service organizations that help define our town, such as delivering Meals-On-Wheels to some of our more needy neighbors.

In short, computers, with their Google-available information and the internet's almost instantaneous circulation of world news, have made possible for us a rare and wonderful new environment. And even for the technically inept senior population unable to take full advantage of all the internet has to offer, very much more is still available. There are enough groups and tasks and pleasures surrounding us in our later years to fill our days and our lives without ever having learned the difference between the iPad, the iPod and the Pea-Pod. Learning the details of this baffling new internet hardware may put us no closer to the expertise of our children and grandchildren, but simply pursuing adequacy in this new technology could help fill our days—and at the very least might be enough to convince our kids that we are not yet altogether obsolete.

And maybe then we should begin to teach them the value of some of the goals and activities that their new technology seems to have replaced.

Our Aging Selves And Nation

As youngsters we were generally so focused on ourselves, on the routine trivia of our emerging lives, that we had little time or interest in examining the conditions of our larger society.

With age and maturity that started to change. For me the transformative moment was the bombing of Pearl Harbor. I had no idea where it was or what it meant, but I was old enough and sensitive enough to the changed and charged climate of our people to recognize the gravity of it. I began to notice that the world was larger and much more complex than I had earlier understood.

Now I and those other Pearl Harbor-era children are seniors—not necessarily wiser, but with a lot more experience under our belts. And now, reflecting on questionable choices we had made over the years, we have become less confident in our judgment, a bit less certain of our insights, and a lot less sanguine about the future of our nation. So now it's time to pause and ask who are we as a people and what do we want?

We think we know who we are—sort of. As children of the Constitution and its subsequent two-hundred-plus years of building on the promises of that document and on the dreams spawned by its vision of concern for "the welfare of the people" and on its democratic principles of equality for all our people, we are the hope of the world and the template for the future. Sort of.

In a sense we are an amalgam of all the people from all the times of history—wise and foolish, talented and inept, selfish and philanthropic. We are the history of Man. But here in America we are also keepers of a flame lit by our revolutionary ancestors—the successors to and continuing spirit of a dream. For most of us, of course, financial and emotional security are our most central focus, but the spirit of community continues to play a role in our lives and remains a part of our heritage, the essence of the spirit of our traditions.

Or it did until recently.

To some degree, of course, the pursuit of self-interest is the natural drive for us all, but self-indulgence is not our distinguishing feature. Whether it is our natural instincts or lessons learned from traditions established by our Constitution and reinforced by the generations that first followed, we as a nation had always honored higher aspirations, wishing the very best for our fellows and willing to sacrifice some of our well-being to help the most needy among us. That is the essence of our national character, calling as it does for a focus on We the People's pledge to "Promote the general Welfare . . . ."

Trouble is, that is not an effective campaign issue. Because of the connection between the provision of aid and its cost, most candidates for political office will not touch it and too many of our citizenry would rather not think about it. Plotting and pursuing a future for ourselves and our families is, of course, a necessary and honorable role, but as a relatively secure and sensitive people who are products of the higher principles defined and demanded by our Constitution, we had and still have a more comprehensive and humane outlook than simply increased accumulation of assets.

The larger tragedies of nature—the Katrina hurricanes, the massive California firestorms, the horrors of the Japanese earthquake and tsunami—grab our hearts and our charitable instincts, but the more common, while equally tragic, collapse of indigent individuals is met with hesitation and calculation. After affixing a price for remediation, our thoughts turn to taxes as the means of payment—an unpopular topic for a constituency always a bit short of funds even if secure. That is when our instinct for compassion is transformed into a political struggle against Big Government, fearful of its power to levy taxes, but dismissive of the benefits—even the necessities—made possible by those taxes.

Unfortunately, that interpretation of motives and actions frustrates the higher aspirations of our founding principles and the more charitable instincts of our people. As with the dramatic tragedies of natural disasters, the individual's more devastating pains of poverty must also be met and resolved, and although the details of funding play a serious role in meeting the challenges of relief, they are not at the top of the list. "Planning for the long run" is a popular and efficient factor in running a society, but for today's hungry and homeless and hopeless—and for the elderly and ill without a path to the future—the "long run" is today. We must first attend the survival needs of the needy—then talk about taxes tomorrow.

Because that is who we are.

Our Endangered Legacy

One of the notable features of aging is our tendency to examine the past with eyes firmly (if falsely) focused on "the good ol' days"—those questionably pleasurable and productive times of our youth. At times, however, those reflections drift away from reality and into fading daydreams built on some unlikely memories from our youth or some imagined glories of our origins.

All four of my grandparents, like the parents and grandparents of almost all the kids I knew, immigrated to this country from the impoverished villages of eastern Europe. They came without money, without the language, without connections—with nothing but hope. They struggled and they survived, but mainly—the biggest triumph of all—they were now Americans.

As a new nation still struggling to its feet in 1787, our constitution outlined its Founders' hopes and purpose in a Preamble that pledged to "establish Justice [and] promote the general Welfare," a noble commitment for a people facing continuing hostilities from both the Old World and the New . . . and the distress of an economy not yet working . . . and the uncertainty of traditions not yet established. Over the next two-plus centuries the hostility diminished, the economy blossomed and the traditions grew and glowed to the admiration and envy of the whole world.

Unfortunately, this glorious land of milk and money is slowly losing its way, forfeiting the nobility of its broad humanitarian concerns in exchange for cutting costs and reducing taxes. The "better life" is an admirable goal, but we have become so focused on economic efficiency and the mechanics of governance that the principles shaped by our Founders and articulated in our Constitution now seem increasingly inconsequential. A balanced budget is a reasonable component of good government, but it should be part of the *mechanics* of governance—not its purpose. The Reagan slogan that "government is not the solution—government is the problem" still resonates with much of our population, but it fails to address concrete problems affecting the lives of many of the more disadvantaged of our people, or to adhere to the principles of our Constitution, and it bypasses many of the traditions we cherish.

The almost comic insistence of President Calvin Coolidge that "the business of government is business" is rapidly becoming established fact. Our expanding profit-and-loss motivation is changing the way our country functions, substituting corporate efficiency for human sensitivity. Lost, or at least seriously diminished, is the concept of pride as a motive for serving our nation and our neighbors, thereby helping to remake our country from a nation of "We the People . . ." into a Board of Directors overseeing its investments.

It is natural and proper for us to focus on our own well-being, both immediate and long-term, but there must still be room within ourselves and our society for those in serious need. While many of our more needy neighbors remain poor and jobless and without adequate benefits of medical or educational or nutritional care, the growing wisdom is that first we must improve our economy to afford such charity, that we must first "get our own house in order." Unfortunately, that means that those who need help will simply have to wait their turn. The problem with that approach is that for those citizens dependent on humanitarian assistance for survival— medical, shelter, food—there may not be the time left to wait for an economic upturn.

As a senior looking back on the more glorious pieces of our past, I like to believe that the nobility of those people is reflected in who we are today—that the people at the core of our nation remain the same generous and concerned citizens they were at the beginning.

Habitat For Humanity, for example, providing shelter for many millions of desperate people worldwide, is constructed and financed by our neighbors. And The Peace Corps is over-subscribed with idealistic young volunteers. And Bill Gates pushed himself out of competition for world's richest individual by giving away $53 Billion of his own money to assorted charities.

I realize that, along with most seniors, I tend to romanticize the past—both mine and my country's—but while those memories may be flawed, they are an essential and enriching part of our history. Idealizing our past may not be a commendable fabrication, but it does help define some of the true glory of our legacy. We the People do still care, but our system is becoming less reflective of our character.

Meanwhile, we seniors, even as a fading minority with muted voices, might still have an impact. Our kids and grandchildren often confuse our longevity with wisdom, so they may accept our contention that it was the high principles and rich Constitutional values that had shaped our country. With luck that just may be enough to inspire their generation and the next to follow a similar path.

Our Separation Complex:
From Work To Leisure

Properly nurtured, age can lift a wine from palatable to exotic, can transform casual passion into eternal love, can convert a sap-soaked bug into a fossilized treasure. On the other hand, that same time lapse can turn good wine into vinegar and cause prime meat to rot. To a large extent the outcome of the process is up to us.

The phenomenon of Old Age is one of the most feared and misunderstood periods in the schedule of man, which is a shame. Oh sure, young, strong and immortal, as are most youngsters short of seniorhood, is preferable, but there is also a lot to be said for old age—except that it doesn't last long enough. Even aside from such fringe benefits as being offered a seat on a crowded bus or getting discounts at the movies and golf courses, there are pleasures in aging that are not ordinarily available to those 40 - to 50-year-old kids who tremble in fearful anticipation of growing old. With aging, for example, comes the freedom of retirement supported by a Social Security income and maybe something more from an employment pension fund. Also reflected in that changed lifestyle, however, is a greatly reduced schedule of activities, inviting boredom or depression to help fill the gap. What is needed, then, are new challenges, new patterns to replace old routines. Now that we have the opportunity to pursue those activities that had been beyond our reach during those years on the job, we should take advantage of our new freedom by learning new skills or seeking new destinations or experimenting with new techniques.

Age does have its problems, of course, but how we deal with our new identity and adjust to our new milieu is largely up to us. We can continue our new lives in our old patterns, or we can seek new experiences, new skills and new interests to replace our expired routines. The transition to senior status should not simply be a reconfiguration of an old lifestyle, but should represent a new period in our old life and be enjoyed in that context.

The most common complaint of my contemporaries—aside from arthritis and failing memory and income anxiety and similar such problems of age-related deterioration—is boredom. In the past we were constantly challenged—to earn a living or shape our kids or please our boss or whatever. Now we no longer have a job, our kids are busy trying to shape their kids, our boss has retired and moved to Florida—and now it is time for us to move on. Most of us have a list of neglected activities that had teased us during decades gone by, those days when full-time obligations prohibited us from devoting any time to the pursuit of personal pleasures. Now, having reached the more distant end of the aging process, we have the time to pursue those missed desires and experiment with more challenging pastimes—and without any dispiriting feelings of guilt.

For some of us, full participation in what we remember of our more active pursuits might be impeded by our aging bodies. Simply being mobile around the house and conversant with daytime TV is not enough, so we must adjust to our new constraints. It is meeting the challenges of the coming days that keep us going. We should find ways to be productive, even if that productivity produces nothing. Building flower boxes in our basement workshop can be a fulfilling experience, or improving our golf game, or learning a new language—anything that requires personal involvement and yields tangible results, however inconsequential those results might be.

A good example of meeting this new challenge of excessive free time is shown by my friend Ron who had spent his preceding half-century in medical school—first learning, then practicing and teaching, finally retiring to his books and his collection of classical records. For some, reading good books and listening to good music is enough, but Ron needed a bit more stimulation, so upon retirement and without any previous experience Ron bought a violin, hired an instructor and began his Phase Two of life. Now, after several years of lessons and practice, Ron plays with an amateur string quartet each weekend and cannot wait for each new day to begin.

For most of us it is this contemplation of what comes next, the anticipation of new challenges, perhaps new successes or even new failures to be overcome, that keeps us going. Our more unsettling concern is the prospect of a future without value or consequence.

And those who fear the end of days without substance or interest need have no concern—many opportunities remain open for continuing lives of interest and productivity. Aside from personal new chores and challenges, there are almost unlimited openings for volunteer services in the public sector—driving to serve Meals on Wheels to the homebound, or to help any one of the groups sponsored by the Turner Senior Resource Center, or the Osher Lifelong Learning Institute. The list is almost without end.

In short, quitting is not an option, so we might as well enjoy ourselves now that we have the chance.

Principles: The Path To The Future

"In the beginning . . . " is a great place to start, but we have to agree on when the beginning began. For some humanists it was about the time that Adam lost his rib and his heart to Eve. Many scientists opt for the moment of The Big Bang 15 billion years ago, while a few originalists hold to their own more unique fantasies, such as Bishop Ussher who insisted the world's first day began on a morning in 4004 BC.

Whatever the fact, they share a single truth—there was a beginning, a moment when it all began. The question now is matching the beginning to the issue.

For most Americans, the beginning was part of the immigration process when abused people of other nations sought and found refuge in this strange new land. First it was the Spanish landing in Florida in the early 16th century, followed a century later when the English founded Plymouth Colony and began a system of governance that finally led to the democratic concept that "all men are created equal . . . endowed . . . with certain unalienable Rights [including] Life, Liberty and the pursuit of Happiness." That was the beginning of a whole new era, unique in the history of Man, in which the citizen became the focus and the purpose of government.

And right from the beginning it worked. Washington Irving, even with his deep love of all things British, had to concede that the United States was "a country in a singular state of moral and physical development; a country in which one of the greatest Political experiments in the history of the world is now performing," further praising our devotion to "sound moral and religious principles, which give force and sustained energy to the character of a people."

And that's who once we were. Since then, our pride as a nation sworn to "promote the general Welfare" has redirected its attention from "the welfare of the people" to a program centered on avoidance of taxes. The idealism conceived in a spirit of purity of purpose and with the well-being of our fellows as its central focus, is being transformed into a struggle for personal comfort, with responsibility limited to just ourselves. In a nation this big and this strong and this prosperous, there should be enough benefits left over for all its people.

Unfortunately, our national focus is increasingly about the tactics of governance rather than about the goals or ideals that motivated our Founders and inspired our earliest settlers. Our drive is no longer about what we want as a nation—it is about how much we are willing to pay for it and the least inconvenient way to raise those funds. The argument about healthcare, for example, was more about building our programs of aid according to our inventory of dollars rather than about attending to the basic needs of our people. Those in need of healthcare should be a primary concern of our nation rather than just an incidental piece of the action.

In the several centuries since our founding, our nation has changed—grown older and stronger and richer. But while "the prevalence of sound moral and religious principles" so vigorously lauded by Washington Irving, is still there, it has lost much of its bloom. We are now more populous, more secure and more consequential in world affairs.

Unfortunately, that maturity is changing our character as well as our profile. What once was praised as "one of the greatest Political experiments in the history of the world" is fading, giving way to some of the same sins of insensitivity that had plagued world societies since the earliest days of civilization. Our task now is to refocus on our principles rather than on our personal comforts and limited self-interests. Tax relief is a reasonable concern for all of us, but it should not be central to our performance and our goals.

Those noble principles expressed in the Preamble to our Constitution are being reduced to quaint slogans of little consequence. Our nation stands for much more than "tax relief" and some of the incidental pleasures of affluence. However short of its apparent reality, we really are a nation of idealism, conceived and fashioned in a spirit of purity of purpose. Our achievements, of course, will never reach the glory of our dreams, but those aspirations of our earliest settlers should still be the principles by which we strive to govern.

And even if that reverie is no more solid than Don Quixote's "impossible dream" we are still that much further ahead for simply having set goals a bit higher than "tax reduction"—and is a whole lot closer to who we are as a nation and as a people.

Patience: A Practice With
A Short Future

One of the benefits of aging is the inclination, borne of maturity, to help lengthen the short fuse of youth. Like the kid who misunderstands an innocent comment and views it as a verbal attack and blows. Or the one with a fragile ego who sees a raised eyebrow as an insult and lashes out. We seniors, however, experienced with the vagaries of life, can better understand some of humankind's more outlandish idiosyncrasies and are more inclined toward patience and forgiveness. Some of us. Some of the time.

Occasionally, however, those idiosyncrasies can pose a serious threat to us—to choices we have made or values we have accepted or aspirations we have embraced. I mention this now because of my instinctive reaction to the sight of some teenage boys I passed on the street recently who were in the throes of the latest silly fashion fad—trousers hanging down from the buttocks instead of the waist, the crotch almost dragging along the ground. How they manage to keep them thus suspended is a mystery, but not so the why: it is to harass their seniors.

By now we should understand some of youth's more outlandish peculiarities and be inclined to forgive them. If it were you who complained of it to me I could calmly, confidently and wisely explain that these are children who are (a) protesting aspects of a society with which they disagree, or (b) simply finding a means of expression for their newly emerging independence. It is simply an unfamiliar aspect of their rite of passage into adulthood, into responsibility and sobriety.

Unfortunately, that objective and well-reasoned logic goes for you, but not necessarily for me. (As with most people, my special strength is in dispensing wisdom—not absorbing it.) For a variety of reasons, as we grow older we tend to become less patient with some of the frivolities of youth. Some of it may stem from memories of our own moments of wasted youth, the guilt of having once been young and foolish ourselves—and from the mature realization that time is increasingly short for any sort of mid-term corrections. With our own vistas so much more limited, we are inclined to manage our affairs and dedicate our energies with greater efficiency—or perhaps with a greater fear of lost time. We are anxiously hoarding our limited time and are offended by its waste.

On the other hand, of course, our disdain for the shallow and superficial concerns of youth, carried to its furthest boundary, can be reflected in the comments of Andy Rooney, that self-styled "lovable old curmudgeon" on TV's Sixty Minutes who took umbrage at the suicide of Kurt Cobain, the 27 year-old successful rock star, asking what did that kid have to complain about, insisting that his own generation had The Great Depression and World War II, but we didn't go around moaning and complaining and killing ourselves. "What would all these young people do if they had real problems . . . ?"

The obvious fact, of course, is that individual problems cannot be measured against some acceptable norm—above this line you have our sympathy (but not necessarily our help) and below it . . . get back to work or school or life, you slacker!

The problems of the aged may well be those of life and death, but they are not necessarily more serious than youthful problems of failure or embarrassment or dismissal by parent or authority or friend. Some of the bromides of our youth were designed to teach us compassion and humility, to impress upon us the reality that some parts of society are much worse off than we, such as the Indian Proverb of the lad who was sad because he had no shoes—until he met another who had no feet. (I remember each time I demurred at eating my broccoli or spinach or other unacceptable foodstuff, being lectured by my mother about the poor starving Chinese who would give anything for what I left on my plate. I do not, however, remember feeling any guilt about it).

Which does not, of course, mean that we have to embrace the more bizarre forms of youthful rebellion, merely that we should accept them. The sight of pink spiked hair I can live with, probably because I know it will someday wash out. Nose rings and cheek rings, however, leave me not only uneasy, but seriously puzzled. How in the world does a youngster with a cold mop up after a sneeze? And assuming an attraction between the sexes, how do two people with rings through their lips kiss without their attachment becoming more permanent and more painful?

There is nothing wrong, of course, with falling pants or punctured lips or rainbow-colored hair—just that age sometimes makes us a bit more rigid in our attitudes than is wise or healthy—whether in politics or changing social customs or in personal relationships. The lesson we seniors should take from this is simply that we should never be too old to learn new lessons.

Our One Nation—
Increasingly Divisible

T om Paine, newly arrived from France, saw the times as a test for men's souls. Alexander Hamilton, a young pauper from the West Indies, arrived in time to take that test—and passed. Thomas Jefferson, the wealthy Virginia landowner, and Molly Pitcher, the little girl of Irish poverty—all different, all foreign to one another, but all sharing the same dream of a nation dedicated to Liberty and Equality, belonging to and serving all its people alike.

Those earliest citizens collected their dreams and put them into the preamble of their menu for America, insisting that "We the People . . . establish Justice . . . (and) promote the general Welfare." Never before had such noble purpose and humanitarian promise been the motivating goal of nationhood; never before had a future shone so brightly for a nation of immigrants. Unfortunately, even the highest of principles can in time fade and although those proclamations established the standards and set the traditions that became our national character and by which we, then and still, define ourselves, they are now becoming increasingly less applicable. Fading dreams cannot long stand up to the contrary demands of reality.

And today's reality is that we have run short of cash. After cutting the taxes that support many of the needs of our most needy and using most of what's left to fund a trillion-dollar war (that's a thousand times a billion—beyond the comprehension of most mortals), the means that might give substance to the dream are in dangerously short supply. Criticism of the war is not the intention of this discussion, nor is the cost—merely the warped priorities attending the process. Whatever the cost, the first obligation of a country at war is its military mission, but second and third and still further on down the list is the continuing necessity to fund the basics of governance so that the country will still be a viable nation when that war is won. The health needs of our people must still be attended, and the police must still maintain order, and the potholes must still be filled—at whatever the cost. True, the treasury is not without limit, so if running the war *and* paying for police and fire protection *and* keeping schools and hospitals open cannot be continued in reasonable fashion with the same income, then clearly a better balance between need and delivery must be achieved. There is always room, of course, for improved efficiency, but equally obvious is the need for an increase in our national income, whether by raising income taxes or instituting different kinds of taxes or finding new sources of income altogether. These are all issues of great moment, but they are matters more of *tactics* than of basic philosophy.

World War II broke out during the worst depression in our nation's history, but even without available funds we managed to build a massive, world-class air force and hire millions of soldiers to fire new weapons and ride in new tanks and float on new ships and do all those many things required of a military power. Meeting those demands required dedication and sacrifice—freezing defense workers' salaries, doubling taxes on the middle class, taxing up to 91% of the income of the most wealthy—but we paid for the war, won the war and kept the country operating. Cutting costs to relieve an over-extended budget is sound fiscal policy, but simply transferring that burden onto the shoulders of our least advantaged by cutting back on such welfare benefits as food stamps for the hungry or Head Start for the impoverished or housing assistance for the homeless is irresponsible and makes a shambles of the principles on which our nation was founded.

The very fact of our national concern for setting and meeting standards of care for our least advantaged is testimony to the unique nature of our democracy and is what helps distinguish our country from all others in the world—perhaps even in world history. Our nation's humanitarian needs should be kept immune from the pressures and preferences of the privileged and powerful. There should be guidelines for our actions, but those guidelines must be principled rather than politically convenient. And after 225 years of service, where better to find that principle than in the preamble to our Constitution where We the People pledged to "promote the general Welfare."

To bring funding and need into reasonable balance we have to concentrate on the principles that have defined and inspired our people since our nation's birth—and if its benefits are not available within the limits of the existing budget, revise the budget—not the principle. Those programs that serve our people must not be dismissed when they become inconvenient and if sacrifices are required they should be borne by all our people, privileged and needy alike. In his second inaugural address in 1937, Franklin Roosevelt said, "Government is competent when all who comprise it work as trustees for the whole people"—not a bad definition of principles by which to govern and to live.

Seeing The World Through Aging Eyes

Location, location. For Beauty it's in the eye of the beholder. For those in the atrium of old age it could still be waiting a couple of decades down the line. But for the true seniors closer to the end of that line, the destination is more likely to be found in the mind than on the calendar. I know that Youth is not Eternal and I'm aware of the role that luck, health and genes play in our age-adjusted performance, but as long as we can still perform some of the requisite functions of life, even if inadequately, we should refuse to quit or accede to being put out to pasture as obsolete observers. There is always something more to do or see or experience.

To some degree, the limitations imposed by age can be offset by the new freedoms provided by our longevity. As compensation for the restrictions accompanying our increasing frailty, we can now use our newly freed hours or days of retirement to experiment or learn or simply to enjoy. As our movements become more restricted by age, we should seek compensation by finding new adventures, new experiences, new avenues of expression in whatever way possible. Where those new paths might lead or what form they might take is, of course, a matter of personal taste or uncontrolled happenstance, but the idea of "new" is key. It could be in developing new skills—sculpting, or painting, or playing a musical instrument, or any one of countless other challenges—or it could simply be in contemplating familiar paths of life in entirely new ways. But whatever route is taken, it must be interesting, perhaps exciting, certainly challenging—and new.

For example, late in my career, with no experience and less money, I opened a travel agency. Part of the purpose (aside from replacing the lost source of income from our outdated fabric stores) was the lure of seeing and experiencing those parts of the world that had always been too far outside my grasp. Now, with the agency as both the means and the excuse, my wife and I were able to participate in activities for which we had never before had the time or finances to pursue. Now that our kids were on their own and the mortgage paid, we could take full advantage of those special benefits provided us by our airline and cruise suppliers.

As owners of a new agency, we took our first international trip, ostensibly to learn more about the product we were selling, but really as a pleasure trip using the business as an excuse. As a departure gift our daughter gave us a book of blank pages, for which, as a confused, but loving father, I smiled in gratitude. She further insisted that I keep notes of our trip's details, a demand with which I obediently complied: "We're now in Rome. Staying at X Hotel. Today we saw the Coliseum." etc. But as we saw more and became more fascinated with what we saw and experienced, my descriptions became increasingly more detailed—much more personal and complex. In time I was as interested in my literary descriptions as in the sights prompting them. And that, too, was the beginning of a whole new chapter in our lives. That blank book, demanding much closer attention to what we saw and what we did, helped expand our understanding and appreciation of the experience. As seniors presumably approaching the conclusion of life's adventures, we had inadvertently become novices at the start of a whole new journey.

Despite our personal appetites for new and exciting adventures, however, the reality is that many seniors are often limited in varying degrees by age-related conditions of health and strength. We are not all capable of handling the more challenging requirements of travel, in which case I suggest considering the assistance-related alternatives. Instead of booking your own flights and hotels, then renting a car with which to explore the country, take a pre-packaged tour, leaving the work of travel to others. On several of our trips we came across such tours which included (although not designed for) seriously incapacitated travelers limited to walkers or wheelchairs. I questioned several such travelers to get their reactions and in every case they responded with enthusiasm and pleasure, highly recommending the experience. The conclusion: Infirmity is certainly a handicap, but not necessarily a reasonable basis or an acceptable excuse for inactivity.

The mistake so many of us make is in giving in to the problems of age, not by recognizing our frailties, but by concentrating on them and thereby accepting new, but not always necessary or valid, restrictions. Admitting reality is sensible and mature, but does not necessarily require surrendering to it.

In brief, "new" is not always good or wise or productive, but if its alternative is a continuation of indolence or a reliance on skills or needs no longer applicable or enjoyable, then it is time to reconsider. All things considered, "new" is a whole lot better than, "You kidding? At my age?"

Finding Our Way

As the son of a retail fabric merchant, one of the pointless memories from my youth was watching the guy in the wholesaler's warehouse estimate yardage by holding one end of the questioned fabric in his fully extended left hand while turning his head to the right and using his nose as the point for a one yard measurement. And it worked—at least for rough estimates and for some of the time. Just don't bet the farm on its accuracy.

And now in our kitchen, by replacing measurements of "a pinch," "a dollop," and "a handful" with "a teaspoon," "a tablespoon" and "a cup," my wife's brownies and apricot coffee cakes are more likely to be mind-boggling than merely outstanding.

All of which emphasizes the need for standards by which to plan our efforts and draft our future rather than by simply using gut-feelings of good or bad or possible. And nowhere is the need for thorough, realistic planning more consequential than in planning the rules and regulations by which to govern our nation. And that is the trouble with our current approach to the basic problems of governance. We tend to start by choosing between our personal pleasures and aversions, then designing our nation's future according to those prejudices. But that just won't work.

Our political extremists, for example, are gaining strength on the basis of the fears they project or the Nirvana they fantasize. They are passionately against big government and big budgets, but rarely voice anything more substantive than vague slogans of hope and hate. Their most unifying anger is the discomfort of taxes and their most motivating fear is of future tax increases, but they offer no alternative source of funding beyond doing without. They have no plan or analysis of how society might work without the assistance of taxes to fund our police and fire departments, or to keep our highway system intact and military strong, or how to keep our libraries and public education up to date and operating.

In short, they may be earnest, but too many tend to be short-sighted with no idea of what comes next, and no vision of what the future might portend. It is probably true that today's political extremists will have little lasting influence and a short life, but they are symptomatic of our nation's dwindling goals and changing values—and that bodes badly for the next round. There must be accepted and reliable criteria by which to judge our values and choose our goals. There must be an identifiable set of principles by which to build our nation and measure our progress—a measurement more studied than simply not liking taxes. Otherwise, decisions for all our society and our children and the future of our nation will be made according to the short-term personal idiosyncrasies of those who are charged with planning and enforcement, rather than by the ideals which should be our guide.

And we do have such a guide, the original one embedded in the introduction to our Constitution. Unfortunately, for many of our more radical electorate (right or left), the guide to our national purpose and character seems to be overlooked or dismissed as grossly outdated. The Preamble, they will note, has not a single reference to excessive taxation, nor does it mention gay marriage or welfare mothers or abortion rights. Nor, of course, should it. The Preamble is concerned with the direction and obligations of our society, with the goals and aspirations of our society. It is those goals that define our nation—the goals, not the tactics of achieving them—that make us unique in all world history. If our taxes are too high or our programs inefficient or our views outdated, then correct them—revise them—improve them. But we must not just dismiss them, allowing them to fade as a consequence of disinterest or oversight. Taxes, after all, are simply a tactic, a way of paying for programs that we have chosen and that define us.

Most of us, even the more conservative among us, tend to support the principles proclaimed in our Constitution's Preamble—those principles that have made our nation so great and respected and strong. We have pledged to *"establish Justice, insure domestic Tranquility . . . promote the general Welfare"*—and that is who we are. When we welcomed to our shores the world's "tired, poor . . . and huddled masses yearning to breathe free" we succeeded in becoming our own greatest beneficiaries, growing ever larger in spirit and understanding, becoming the greatest symbol and source of hope in all world history.

And now we are in serious danger of allowing it all to just drift away. We are so offended by taxes, for example, that we ignore the national pain and hardship that would be the consequence of their elimination, or the problems of our society that found relief through the imposition of those taxes, and simply focus on the elimination of that single source of discomfort. Rather than retreating into our cocoon of comfort we should perhaps struggle to improve the efficiency of our system, not to abandon all the glory that had been ours and that had once defined us. The ever widening space between our nation's needy and ourselves, our decreasing concern with the welfare of neighbors who are not family, is a dangerous symptom of our decline.

Optimism: Playing Against The Odds

I have always been a little lax on logic, relying instead on a combination of instinct and hope—which is a great formula for disaster. I realize, for example, that investments should be based on a careful evaluation of the likelihood of success, or by balancing the estimated return against the risks, or at least with consideration of the potential long-term value that may be inherent in the venture. It should certainly not be made simply on the high hopes or foolish dreams of rank amateurs—which tends to be my style.

We don't always have enough control over our emotions, however, to follow that course. And sometimes the problem is more genetic than intellectual—simply who we are as opposed to the strength and wisdom of the character to which we may aspire. I'm thinking of that time many decades ago when my mother in New Jersey called me at my store in Ann Arbor and left a message for me to call her as soon as I returned. She then tried one of my other stores, leaving the same message. Then left a message on my home phone to call her back. By the time I finally uncovered her many messages I was very close to panic, manufacturing crises in my mind that included all the worst forms of disaster—irremediable illness, debilitating accident, devastating tragedies growing increasingly worse. And was it a problem affecting my mother or another member—perhaps members—of my family. I finally got her on the phone and breathlessly asked what was wrong? How was she? How was everyone else?

"Oh, nothing's wrong. I just got a really good stock tip and wanted to pass it on. San Juan Racetrack! Two-fifty a share and I hear it's really good." It was, of course, dead within a couple of weeks—as nearly was I. But she tried hard and meant well and that's all we can expect from those near and dear to us.

My game of poker falls into a similar pattern of disregard for caution or logic—much to my dismay. The book written by my late friend, Peter Steiner, examines the scientific odds of hitting a full house when holding trips (three of a kind) and advises balancing the risk (the size of the bet) against the anticipated return for that investment. Unfortunately—no, foolishly!—I'm too often blinded by anticipation of the full-house promised by the turn of the next card, conveniently dismissing the costly disaster waiting in the wings.

In an entirely different milieu is the irrational way I too often play my game of golf. I am somewhat less than a skilled player, but much more damaging is the blind sense of optimism I bring to it. For example, with a creek or lake shining midway between my golf ball and the green, the wise procedure for an inadequate player would be to play just short of the water, then take a short pitch onto the green with the next shot, or perhaps to aim off to the side of the water hazard so as to be wide of the green, but dry. Or, of course, there is the third approach—midstream in the creek or in the center of the lake—which has less appeal, but is more familiar.

The point of all this is that for irrational optimism there is a price to be paid, but an argument can be made that the rewards could be equally outsized. A continuing sense of remorse for foolish and costly errors of judgment—such as investing heavily in San Juan Racetrack—deserves serious personal reproach, but it is difficult to redesign the player after decades of malfunction.

The reality, of course, is that we are built according to formulae over which we had little or no control. Whether because of our genes or because of the manipulation of our character by parents or circumstances during our early years, or simply following the fatalism expressed by our 1920's philosopher, Popeye, who noted that, "I yam what I yam and that's all that I yam," the fact is that who we now are is who we have always been.

Which is an unacceptable excuse for doing nothing to improve our performance or ourselves—many of our pleasures are derived from having met and conquered adversity—but it is a reasonably relaxing way to live with some of our personal flaws. Living through seven or eight decades gave us plenty of opportunity to err in ways both serious and trivial, but that, too, was part of our nature and education. If it is not too late to make amends for some of our misguided actions we should do so now, but at some point we must move on.

Perfection is certainly a worthy goal, but none of us falls into that category—and now making peace with reality is not such a bad way to continue to go through life.

Seniors And Senoritas

Lena Driskell, a seventy-nine-year-old great-grandmother, lived in a nursing home in Atlanta with her boyfriend, eighty-five-year-old Herman Winslow. All was working just fine until she discovered that he was playing around with another woman . . . so she shot him.

When reported in the press, the issue that most puzzled the readers was more the bizarre nature of the action than the crime itself. What in the world could have precipitated and directed such passion and such outlandish behavior in people that old?

Most members of generations younger than very old see antique codgers in their 70s, 80s and beyond as more a different species than simply a different generation. How, after all, can people that age have relationships other than grandparental. Youngsters (by which I mean short of their mid-fifties) with that phase of life still in their distant future, don't seem to understand that the really old are simply ordinary people who have lived longer—perhaps a lot longer.

Advanced age does not relieve us of the legal or moral obligations of civil behavior, but neither does it mean the transformation from who we were when young into a stranger formulated by the accumulation of years. The flaws and strengths and idiosyncrasies of our youth, if part of our character then, remains with us as we grow old—even very old. Shooting your ex-lover is not the best way to even the score—just that the aches of the "cheatin' heart" of song and story hold much the same place in our senior years as they did when we were young. Seniors haven't changed all that much—their interests, their needs, even their passions remain a continuing part of their lives. The only adjustment is that as seniors they now move at a slower pace. There are other ways to deal with the disappointments of life, methods a bit less dramatic or final than the one chosen by Lena Driskell, but solutions for the aged are not that distant from the choices of the young—just tempered somewhat by the lessons absorbed during the journey. We know, for example, that if we live long enough we'll get old and die—a reality alluded to by Groucho Marx when he said, "I intend to live forever, or die trying"—and that's just the way it is. But that inevitability should not design our trip or tailor the way we get there.

Even though Lena Driskell had reached the edge of aged (still only on the edge in the biased eyes of this 85-year-old reporter) and was living in a retirement home, there is no reason to assign her to the dustbin of life. Some of the enthusiasms and pleasures —and miseries and fears and flaws—of life may have dimmed since her earlier years, but the essence of her youthful demons and desires remain a focus of her life. And that's the way it should be—although I do recommend a more restrained performance. Shooting an unfaithful mate may well let off steam, but that relief—like poor Herman Winslow—will probably be short-lived.

The misguided perceptions of youth that view the old as vacuous and out of the loop often shape the views of our older selves when we too reach that stage, so that while we may see ourselves as beyond the passions and the challenges of life, we may in reality still have still have pleasures to be pursued and lessons to be learned and adventures and discoveries still to be explored.

And that is the point of this ramble. Despite the presumptions of the young, old people are not different creatures. They . . . we . . . are simply somewhat faded examples of who we once were. The pleasures and aspirations that had motivated us to better meet the future are still the driving forces in our lives. The interests and goals of our youth may have changed form, but not essence. The more energetic activities of football and basketball, for example, have been replaced by the more equable challenges of golf (using a cart), and we may have matured from immersing ourselves in paperback murder mysteries into studying the mysteries of ancient history, but all of that is part of our growth, part of our maturation—not of our transformation. With age our paths and positions may have changed, but we remain who we were—only older.

And that means that our passions for life may not be as heated as earlier, and our energy may not sustain our curiosity for as long as we wish, but the essence of our nature tends to play out its role regardless of the time lag. Whatever Lena Driskell had been earlier in life, whatever pleasures had moved her and whatever fears or needs had limited her, for better or worse, she was still Lena Driskell.

A Senior's View Of Who We Are

One of the benefits of adding even more years to our inventory, aside from still being available to use them and alert enough to deal with them, is the pleasure of recounting the earlier ones to impress the generations behind us. To some of today's kids we may seem like little more than fossils, so we occasionally try to impress them with the more dramatic—and often highly exaggerated—tales of the hardships we had to endure on our way up.

An example is the reaction to the winter's accumulation of snow. In my day, as I explained to my children and grandchildren, I had to walk to and from school through snow piled up to my chin. Of course, it was really only up to my waist and at that age my waist was where my knees are today, but it served its purpose—they were impressed.

Aside from the self-serving fantasies of the storyteller, the differences and the difficulties of some of the times gone by are very real and often quite stunning. As seniors, we often dwell on events that were unique to our youth, thereby bathing our memories in the color and thrills of those experiences. But some of those memories are more real, more substantive, than others.

In the period of the early 1940s, for example, we were emerging from the devastation of the. The Great Depression in time to fight the war in Europe. The war was new and exciting and we were young and anxious for adventure. Our lives were so deeply entangled with the war news from the front and war talk on the radio and war politics in every newspaper and war graphics on the Pathé News and the March Of Time that all of us, whether involved with military matters or simply observers on the outside looking in, were in some sense part of the action.

Living in Trenton, New Jersey, for example, I remember the city blocking all traffic in the center of town to allow for a celebration of the war effort—promoting the sale of war bonds and accepting citizen contributions of such needed war materials as scraps of metal and bits of rubber, even empty toothpaste tubes—for what purpose I still don't know. In one way or another, whether by fighting or by contributing time or money, or simply by cheering those who did, it was our war—we were all connected to it—and we all were very proud.

Well, the times have changed. In those earlier times, most of the tragedies and discomforts of war were shared by us all, but in recent decades that sense of community has been revised. Our society has a new profile. It is still our war, our nation's war, but it is no longer shared by us all—and that is part of the problem. For the families of those fighting and dying, the horrors of the war could not be more real or more devastating, but not all segments of our society share that participation equally. Victory is still the ultimate objective, but close behind is the resolution of the cost factor—how much will it cost and who will pay for it? Some of our biggest and most profitable corporations, for example, have shifted the address of their corporate headquarters to offshore tax-relief havens—even while collecting such rewards as non-competitive military contracts from the government.

The problems of our economy are very serious and must be addressed, but that address must be directed to all of our people— middle class and corporate citizens alike. As of the moment the larger burden is being directed toward the less advantaged middle- and lower-class citizenry. The bulk of our economic balancing act is centered on reducing funds already allocated to serving the needs of our most disadvantaged, rather than demanding similarly inconvenient or costly sacrifices across the board.

Paul Krugman, the Pulitzer Prize-winning economist, recently wrote that "all the policy focus seems to be on tax cuts . . . so one-sixth of America's workers, all those who can't find any job . . . have, in effect, been abandoned." As a result, our nation, once praised as "one of the greatest Political experiments in the history of the world" is now fading.

Not all seniors, of course, share this view of equal obligations, but we do tend to share a pride in our past, in the glories of our forebears whose hardships and sacrifices helped found and build our nation. Now, with the increasingly limited futures of our own, we are anxious to keep the more noble memories of our nation alive for the next generation and beyond.

Such daydreaming may not have much of an immediate impact on our kids or our country, but further into the future it may help protect the nation's rich traditions of fairness and compassion that is our heritage. So even as seniors with muted voices, by using those voices to make our feelings known we may still have a role to play

Rediscovering The Constitution

After eight-plus decades of searching for the right route for serving my family, my community and my conscience, I find there is no single path. In complex, uncertain times the message from the radical right is very appealing: just trust in the Word of the Lord. A few problems with that: Which word? Whose interpretation? And will it be in the original Aramaic or its English translation?

The problems of modern life are far too numerous and confusing to examine and evaluate each issue in detail, hence the temptation to follow the simple path of unquestioned Faith. For some, however, something more concrete is needed to identify and evaluate our nation's higher and more beneficial standards of performance. We need a solid base on which to fashion goals for society, something more reliable, for example, than seductive political promises and comforting sound bites. We need a standard by which to measure the benefits and pitfalls and obligations of legislative proposals.

After well over two hundred years, the Constitution of the United States remains our most honored document, the most reliable echo of the values shaped and articulated by our nation's Founders. It is the promise of that document, among other benefits, to "form a more perfect Union, establish Justice . . . promote the general Welfare, and secure the Blessings of Liberty" that provides the most trusted standard by which to gauge our legislative choices.

By that pledge our government assumed an obligation to care for the basic needs of all its citizens and while the precise nature of those needs may be vague, they must necessarily include food for the hungry, shelter for the homeless, healthcare for the ill and infirm, education for the young, and security for the aged. It is those basic benefits that define the ideals and traditions with which we have gloried and in which we and the generations before us have taken such pride, and it is in the continuing pursuit of those goals that our legislation must focus. Tax reduction, for example, has universal appeal and legislators dare oppose it at their peril, but measured against the blessings envisioned in our founding document's solemn pledge of support for maintaining the well-being of the people, such opposition becomes responsible rather than expedient. Upholding the lofty goals of our Constitution by providing for the needy, too often dismissed as Liberal giveaways, is fully in keeping with the highest standards of the Constitution and is a proud reflection of our nation's humanitarian principles.

In 1944 President Franklin Roosevelt suggested an all-inclusive "Second Bill of Rights," designed to help all the people of the country. Nestling next to remedial programs for the disadvantaged was "the right of every businessman, large and small, to trade in an atmosphere of freedom from unfair competition and domination by monopolies at home or abroad." Roosevelt's intention to aid and protect the needy and the more privileged alike echoes our nation's original goal of creating a truly democratic and inclusive society in which all the people share in the hopes and benefits of freedom, one in which even the least fortunate can enjoy the benefits of a supportive and caring government.

Lately, we have been drifting into a nation of intolerance and greed, with Liberals and Conservatives pursuing different and contradictory agendas. In hopes of political gain, the Democrats have been soft-peddling their tradition of support for the most needy, while the Republicans, by definition and tradition a party "disposed to preserve existing conditions and institutions," has been increasingly focused on improving the welfare of its more powerful and vociferous supporters. By redirecting the country's philosophic goals and legislative efforts away from "the general Welfare," the primary losers would, of course, be the nation's most poor and disadvantaged citizens, but joining them as victims would be our gloried reputation as a haven for "the wretched refuse of our teeming shore" . . . and with it our country's proud and beloved tradition seeking equality and justice for all.

Our need is to reexamine the words and purpose of the Constitution to keep its promise alive, to ensure the continuity of a philosophy and programs of help that only a compassionate and sympathetic government can provide. Those values that had for so long made our nation the envy of the world and the pride of our people are fading. Much political rhetoric is made of "moral values" by which is meant the narrow issues of gay marriage and abortion and public prayer, but little is noted of the larger moral values of satisfying the basic needs of survival for all our people according to the intent and authority of the Constitution. Rather than backing away from these debates we, both liberals and conservatives, should aggressively assume authorship of the true principles of "moral values" and challenge its detractors to define them differently.

The constitutionally mandated compassion of American democracy is perhaps unique in legislative history and has always been a major source of pride among our people, but that pride is turning to shame for some, fear for many, and is being redefined by others. Our obligation now is to reexamine our Constitution and recommit to the humanitarian goals and lofty principles that are its legacy.

A Softer Side Of War

Facing me on the wall of my office is the front page of the *New York Times* from Sunday, March 30, 2003, featuring a photograph of a group of American GIs just standing around—talking, relaxing after a recent military exercise, perhaps preparing for a new one. The center of the picture, in a space left vacant by the other soldiers, shows an American Marine—not the tall, strong, heroic figure of military tradition, but simply middle-aged, balding, overweight—sitting on the ground with a recently orphaned four-year-old girl cradled in his arms. The expressionless child seems comforted by the support and attention of the sober-faced GI. They are two more victims of war, separated from the world, but attached to each other—he with anguish about the trauma facing this newly orphaned child and with evident concern about how she will now cope with life. And she, lost in the vacuum of events she cannot understand, seems content with the love and security of this big man who will protect her and care for her.

And I keep this picture in constant view, because his compassion, his concern for this unknown, unrelated child is largely who we are.

And I remember, too, the picture that appeared in the Times not long afterward of a two-year-old Iraqi boy dying from a 12-pound tumor, almost the size of the child, bulging from his frail body. The child, named Safa'a, is scared and suffering and confused. After a year of inadequate treatment in Iraq, his tumor has squeezed his liver, kidney and intestines all to the side, leaving him in uncontrolled pain and immobility. His trembling, tear-stained mother, sitting scared in a medical center in Jordan, cradles him in her arms while his father, in total despair, tells the newsman, "You know, he is my first baby. I used everything I have to rescue my baby. I tried to do something, but I can't." The inadequate medical skills available in Iraq to treat the boy were further impaired by the sectarian violence that strained the environment—the family is Sunni and the hospital was under the control of a radical Shiite militia.

The picture was taken in Jordan because a liquor distributor in Boston, Mr. Ray Tye, founder of the Ray Tye Medical Aid Foundation, became aware of the tragedy, arranged for the transportation of the child and both parents to the hospital in Jordan, then paid for the five-hour operation that removed the tumor and saved his life. And leaving the hospital for their return to Iraq the photographer captured the immense joy of the moment, the child smiling and happy and both parents overwhelmed with tears of joy and gratitude.

And this, too, on a much broader screen, is who we are.

It is a well known fact that "War is hell"—but that "hell" is not necessarily limited to the battlefield. In a recent op-ed piece by Nicholas Kristof, he had just finished interviewing a few families in Sudan where they are fighting their own kind of war. "We've had nothing to eat but leaves from trees" said one young mother whose son was chewing on a piece of wood. Kristof viewed that hell as "the mass atrocity of a government starving its people, massacring them, raping them, and bombing them." And if he was not writing from Sudan it could well have been from Bahrain—or Somalia—or Rwanda—or, tragically, so many other similarly distressed lands.

But not all the individuals in those assorted Hells are Satan's compatriots. Such examples of humanitarian concern and assistance as those which introduced this article are reasonably accurate reflections of who a large part of our population really are. These acts of blind benevolence help define the character of many of our people, following traditions established by the Founders in their document pledging to "form a more perfect Union . . . promote the general Welfare, and secure the Blessings of Liberty." In a world largely defined by the power of its military and the production of its oil and the Glory of its Leaders, that Preamble is not a bad collection of goals.

Unfortunately, the realities of life are not always kind to our more noble fantasies. The vast sea of violence that colors our front pages and TV news channels overrides the examples of generosity that we like to believe defines us. Nevertheless, those people and organizations—the volunteers who bring food and medicine to decimated villages and those who rebuild housing destroyed by natural disasters and those who build schools for the poorest and most needy children of the world—are much the model for how much of the world sees us. And those redeeming acts of charity, however infrequently noted, are significant and inspiring and remain a recognized and celebrated part of our profile.

We seniors, who have largely been relieved of the tasks and responsibilities of caring for our unrelated needy brethren can do more than a little to help push and promote such deeds of humanitarian care exemplified by those instances noted above. And such participation can go very far in making our longevity a satisfying conclusion and more a blessing than an inconvenience.

Stretching The Brain's Waves

It is a well-known fact that physical exercise is one of the more valuable, more stimulating activities to be inflicted upon Man. Midday naps are good and eating between meals isn't bad, but they cannot hold a candle—or a calorie—to lifting and stretching in order to build a body trim and a stomach flat. There is nothing quite like a physique shaped by the continuing flow of exercise weights lifted and body-weight dropped.

But that does little for the waves of the brain. The boredom of the treadmill can stimulate the heart and dumbing down with dumbbells can beef up the biceps, but that leaves the resident neurons of the brain just lying around with nothing to do beyond listening to music and watching television and growing ever fatter and more lax.

Exercising the brain involves less obvious manipulation of that organ than does a workout on the more visible parts of the body, but maneuvering the mind by weighing words, revising thoughts, and occasionally reversing direction does have a highly beneficial impact on its efficiency and well-being. Challenging old ideas and considering new directions and redesigning old thoughts to reflect new approaches and analyses stimulates the brain in ways that protects and expands its function to the benefit of its host body. Such mental activity invigorates the brain cells in much the same way that physical exercise trims the body fat.

Unlike physical exercise, active thought causes no sweat and need not provoke the pain of strain, but it can significantly change the way the eye sees and the mind examines. In short, in order to stay strong and healthy in attitude and outlook, the mind needs exercise in much the same way as do the muscles of the body. And that is one of the seriously overlooked requirements of seniorhood. Surviving the earlier stages of life and transitioning into the next had required some degree of planning and perseverance, but now—comfortable in what Aesop describes as the seventh and last stage of life—we need no longer struggle. Simply moving on comes naturally and easily. We've grown into that wonderful period of self-indulgence, that plateau of life in which we need not concentrate on being productive, responsible adults. We need answer to nobody but ourselves.

Which sounds very inviting, but answering to nobody but ourselves still requires that we answer. Just closing our eyes and shutting down, ignoring the state of the world, or the problems of our society, or the needs of our fellows will not do it. For very personal, selfish reasons—even aside from moral obligations—we must participate, in the affairs of our community or in our much smaller artificial world of hobbies and personal pastimes. Our body needs its mind and our mind needs its activities.

The largest field of opportunities for mental expansion lies in literature's broad range of challenges. Reading can be among the most satisfying, stimulating mental activities available to all seniors, regardless of background or intellectual skills or interests. Whether the subject is the founding of our nation, or the obscurities of ancient history seen through the eyes of Thucydides, or finding favor in the fables of Aesop, or tingling with the titillation of paperback novels, the stimulation of reading and reacting and remembering is as beneficial as it is pleasurable.

Or join with a friend in similar need of mental stimulation and learn to play chess or bridge or other such competitive intellectual games. Whether you win or lose each subsequent contest, you will have gained immensely from the pleasure and the competition. And even for ancient octogenarians (pardon the personal), learning such new skills as playing a musical instrument, or managing such productive hobbies as woodworking, or painting, or sewing and knitting can provide valuable and fulfilling alternatives to the dangers of quiet self-absorption.

Several years ago, visiting the home of a young relative, I stumbled upon a group of senior men (guests of his father) who had gathered in his house for their monthly meeting. They had all retired after many years of routines that had occupied all their time and thought and energy. With little to do, little left to challenge their mind or occupy their time and feeling superfluous, they joined a cooking class. A cake baking class. When I walked in they were showing off the current monthly results of their newly acquired expertise—a collection of the most beautiful, ornate and delicious cakes I have yet come across. But the quality of the product is not the point—it was the immense pleasure and satisfaction that accompanied their accomplishment that was the victory.

In short, what and how well the challenges are met are of little consequence. It is the stimulation of challenge and growth—possibly enriched by some small degree of success—that is the golden ring on the merry-go-round of age that rewards us all.

Finding A New Compass

With the passage of time I become increasingly conscious of the limitations of age. The realization that people in their seventies and eighties have trouble keeping up with their middle-age counterparts is hardly new or surprising, but now the matter has become personal.

I remember reading the Business section of the Sunday *New York Times* some years ago and coming across an article on Charles Scott, the head of Saachi & Saachi, the giant European advertising agency. The single item of his biography that jumped out at me was the fact that he had been born in 1949. 1949!!! I had already long since returned from military service, narrowly escaped several marriages and was half way through college and he—who was now the hugely successful head of a massive international corporation—was just being born.

Countering that disclosure just two pages later in the same section of that newspaper was an article on James Michener, an active professor at the University of Texas. Among other things, in 1947 he had won a Pulitzer Prize for his collection of stories, "Tales of the South Pacific," from which the musical "South Pacific" was later made. Two years before the birth of that Scott kid, he himself was already grandly successful and now, at the age of 87, was still working, still productive, still a star.

The complex and depressing sense of jealousy and inadequacy fostered by the first article gave way at least somewhat to the glimmer of hope encouraged by the second—that I still had time to make my mark.

All of this bears on my changed status—from a struggling entrepreneur, husband and father to an observer of much that was and still more that should have been. Reflecting on the ever-narrowing road provokes no regrets, but does encourage me to change the pattern of my life, to expand my horizons a bit beyond my personal pleasures and perhaps to seek some new goals, pursue some new achievements. When I was approaching retirement I was thrilled at the prospect of the freedom and relaxation it would provide—but I was wrong. Retirement offered instead a whole new agenda with a radically different set of tasks and responsibilities and opportunities. The difference was to be in the nature of my new life's goals and hopes and in my changed role in the affairs of all around me.

Part of my problem, hardly unique to me, is a search for immortality, not as in "life eternal," but as a small part of my legacy. I'd like to be able to leave some piece of myself behind so the world will have been slightly changed—perhaps improved—by my having taken up space here for so very long. I am not yet ready to give up the dream, but the time allotted for its realization is dwindling and at a rapidly accelerating pace.

Dr. Benjamin Spock, guru for the young and fertile and the father of parental guilt, was worried about the current crop of young people, about their inactivity and general malaise, so he wrote a book about it. His concerns were neither profound nor electrifying, but Dr. Spock was then 91 years old! The wonder is not merely that he had written a book, but that his worry was for the kids, for society—not for himself. He insisted that until age 89 (when he presumably fell ill) he never even thought of himself as old—never thought of age at all, so I still have a few years left in which to make my mark.

Many years ago the two ancient Grand Old Men of our synagogue, both of whom were instrumental in founding and then sustaining the institution, were honored for their decades of service. The first recounted his struggles in getting the congregation established and the synagogue built and described the difficulties encountered in keeping it going and growing. It was an achievement of note for which he deserved—and was given—much honor.

The other, Tom Cook, never once referred to the past. He spoke instead of the problems facing the congregation's emerging youth, of the difficulties that lie ahead for all the needy of our own community and for others more distant. He described some existing charitable youth programs and encouraged us to join them and to develop still other programs of support. He spoke of the fears and the hopes facing the young in the coming decades, noting that what had been done in the past for our own less fortunate young people would have to be repeated and perhaps expanded for the generations yet to come. He pleaded that we anticipate some of the problems awaiting the children of the future and seek ways to avoid or relieve some of the pain such trauma might bring.

In his mid-eighties Tom Cook had already achieved some degree of immortality for all that he had done throughout his life, but his deep concerns for improving the lives and relieving the problems facing tomorrow's youth clinched it. Not a bad way to fashion an exit.

The Way It Was

My mother was ten years old when the Wright Brothers flew the first heavier-than-air machine in the history of Man—for a distance of 852 feet. Some decades later that same woman sat with her grandchildren in front of the television screen and watched the astronauts land their rocket ship on the moon.

All in just one lifetime!

Change, of course, is constant and inevitable, but the tempo of change is increasing at an astonishing pace. A science writer recently concluded that we are now at the midpoint of history, that as much has happened since we were born as had happened up to that point since the beginning of time. The few years since I was a child, for example, have brought the magic of ultrasonic flight and the miracle of organ transplants and have all but eliminated polio and smallpox. Such momentous accomplishments, however, mean nothing to my grandchildren who have trouble visualizing a time without television or computer games or shopping malls. Meanwhile, they remain unaware of the experiences and opportunities and pleasures that were replaced by the television and computer games and shopping malls.

I was once told that as we grow older we don't grow wise—we merely reminisce. Reference to the past tends to be the pastime of the old, remembering "the way it was when I was young." But keeping that past alive, even if only in the minds of children, is more than simple recreation—it helps connect the generations and to maintain some sort of personal balance. The better part of half a century ago my children anxiously pressed me for stories of "the good old days," seeking the details of my past life—who I was and what I did. Now my grandchildren are traveling that same road. Those "good old days," of course, were not necessarily so good, but they were ancient and they were different. My grandchildren see them as romantic moments in an adventurous period piece, a time as foreign as it was distant and uniquely mine. They seem to understand that my past is somehow their past and they want to know more—and satisfying that curiosity is now my continuing obligation.

My goal in reducing some of those memories to words on paper is not to chart the progress or decline of recent civilization, but simply to remember and describe the nature of the pleasures and fears that defined the time of my youth. Historically, that was the era of the Great Depression —the long decade of poverty and desperation that affected—often destroyed—not just the economy of the nation, but the lives and souls of its people as nothing before in our history. In time that period of utter hopelessness gave way to the favorable economics of the war and the exhilaration of its triumphs—and finally to the technological revolution that ushered in one of the most productive periods in the history of Man.

None of which meant very much to those of us who were just beginning our tenure. Few of my generation, just kids at the time, could appreciate the consequences of that revolution as it was unfolding. Splitting the atom had no meaning for us, after all, nor did the invention of plastic, nor the discovery of penicillin. All of that merely dealt with matters of survival. It was the availability of empty neighborhood lots that shaped our young lives—the abundance of innocent, non-threatening space that gave us the freedom to play and grow and experiment. Civilization's victory over some of the scourges of society and the emergence of still others has resonance for sociologists and historians, but for my grandchildren the interest is simply in how we lived and played and felt.

Meanwhile, civilization moves on—and the empty lots are gone. What is not gone are the memories those times invoked and it is those memories that help tie my grandchildren to me and me to my earlier years of growth. But there is more. By reviewing those times I help connect my much younger family to their past and to each other and in the process I manage to instill a sense of continuity to my own existence—a valuable and productive alternative to succumbing to the deterioration of an unchallenged aging process.

And that is the very simple purpose of putting pieces of my background into print, to tell my grandchildren what it was like when we were still young enough to be innocent and indestructible—and to enjoy myself in the re-creation of that period. My children have enough trouble trying to understand that I had once been young— for my grandchildren that is a totally incomprehensible concept. The past is gone and many of its players—both friends and family—are dead. By this effort I want to bring it and them back to life for just these few moments, just long enough for my grandchildren to meet them and know them and perhaps to remember them. Recollections of that past should help them to better know from whence they come—and may help me prolong my own role in it just a bit longer.

Those Little Grey Cells Used
To Be Black And White

Old age is not so bad—it's just the aches and the ailments and the deterioration that define and accompany the aging process that can be so disconcerting.

Among the more serious complaints of the procedure is the loss of small pieces of memory that plague us at the most inopportune moments. It may well be, for example, the confusion of trying to figure why I came here to this store or supermarket—what was it that my wife had instructed me to buy? Or the troubling sense of loss in trying to remember the date of our anniversary—or the ages of my grandchildren—or the names of friends when I run into them on the street.

Of course, it's not all that bleak. After all, as seniors we are given greatly discounted prices for the various sporting events and musical performances and the many other community functions available to us, but our inability to remember the teams or the performers or the many details of the program makes that benefit just a little less valuable or satisfying for us. Even more unsettling, perhaps because it is a more common occurance, is our disconnect from the movies we have just seen. Our fading memory, forgetting the names of the performers and details of the production—perhaps even the name of the movie—makes it difficult to discuss the evening's event with our friends or family. We may remember that we liked it, for example, and can highly recommend it, but have since forgotten the plot—or the title—or the names of key members of the cast.

But take heart—relief is on the way. Not that those critical lost brain cells can be restored, but there is now a way to take advantage of the anxiety—to make a game of this deficit, to find a new source of pleasure in our pain. It's a new pastime which promises to eliminate the panic of memory loss and substitute an exhilarating new sense of competitive accomplishment.

It is called, "Name That . . . oh, Whatever!"

It can be applied to any topic in which the participants are interested and it has no designated starting point, but depends instead on the drift of the discussion. During some casual conversation, for example, one participant might refer to an old movie—it was about this guy in the French Revolution, but I don't think he was actually French, he may have been English, and he was really handsome (what *was* his name?) he was a kind of quiet actor (yes, I'm sure he was English), always seemed reserved and very mature (no, not Victor Mature) and he played in a lot of American films and had a deep, well modulated voice (oh, come on, you know who I mean), he died some years ago, I think he played opposite that Swedish actress, what's her name?, who always "vants to be alone", she's the one who played in that old classic in which she takes a long time dying (Carmen? No. Chamomile? No, that's a tea—can't be that).

Meanwhile, the other player can occasionally join in with such well-placed and thoughtful responses as, Oh, you mean that picture where the lady keeps on knitting whenever somebody falls to the guillotine? Yeah, I know who you mean, but I don't think he was really English, I think he was American, but he had a really cultured English accent (Oh, come on now, what's the matter with me?). It wasn't Melvin Douglas? No, he was the one in that picture with that Swedish actress who never talked. I can't remember, but it's on the tip of my tongue, he was always serious and was always the hero and . . . I think it started with an R . . . Raymond? Roger? Roland?—darn, I've almost got it.

One of the great features of this game is that it has no time limit and can occupy hours, even days, without ever going stale. You might call your opponent at one o'clock in the morning, for example, and triumphantly explode "Ronald Coleman" or "Camille," then go back to sleep, happy in the realization that you have conquered still another threat from old age.

But nothing of consequence comes without a price. Be prepared for a counter-call—perhaps that same night when you've just gotten back to sleep—with an equally triumphant, "Tale Of Two Cities" or "Greta Garbo". After all, what's good for the goose, or something, is something for the something—what in the world *is* that expression?

Old Age: A Good Alternative

As a young boy I remember having family dinner while our guest, Jack Funk, talked about the tragedy of a mutual friend who had recently died at age 42—and I remember being stunned by that disclosure. Oh, I could cope with the fact of his death, just not their classification of "tragedy." After all, he *was* 42!

In one way or another, the specter of old age is with us throughout our lives—it's the definition that can be so unsettling, running anywhere from age forty for youngsters, to age sixty or more for those in their thirties. Problem with that last category are the particulars of its membership. The PGA (Professional Golfers Association), for example, assigns the start of seniorhood to kids of 55. For some, such a proclamation can be dismissed as a matter of semantics, but for still active members of the class of true seniors—antique athletes who run full-speed on the tennis court to return anything that bounces within bounds, or who twist their aging bodies into knots to extend the distance of their golf drives, or who flex their arthritic knees in order to ski over every mogul on each snow-covered slope at top speed—being challenged by such underage competitors can be unfair, unreasonable, and deeply damaging to their egos.

On the other hand—so what! Much of the conquest of the demons of the aging process is in the mind, after all, so if we are able to participate in familiar athletic activities at this tail-end of our tenure and to do so at least reasonably well—even with losing—then we're well prepared to attack still another day.

There should be limits, of course, to the drive to inflate our self-image—skydiving and ski-jumping are probably out—but even if competitive exercises do little to postpone the inevitable, they surely do make the moment a lot more palatable. And part of the beauty of trying new things (or old things over again) at this age is the pain-free realization of failure: nobody, including yourself, expects too much, so nobody, including yourself, will be too disappointed by failure. My golf game is the perfect example. Time was that everybody I knew played in the nineties (score, *i.e.*, not age or temperature), struggling for the eighties, which is why my scores in the hundred-plus range won me no friends or game invitations. Now at age eighty-five, bringing my score down to a still embarrassing 100 but anticipating 98 tomorrow is thrilling and satisfying and makes me the hero of the day. All of which pretty much encapsulates the basic strategy of dealing with the problems of age—remembering yesterday is okay if you have nothing better to do, but tomorrow is the new frontier. And while my wife's admonition to "Act your age" is sensible and mature, if it means acquiescing to some of the ugly realities of deterioration, then No thanks. Playing all those games to win—tennis, golf, poker, whatever—is stimulating and fun, but even the pain of losing is mitigated by having made the effort, done reasonably well, and are still breathing on our own . . . albeit in short puffs. Such physical activity won't keep us young—at age eighty-plus we're long since past "young"—but it is satisfying and keeps us looking forward to the next day and the next challenge.

One of the past pleasures of approaching old age was the anticipation of retirement—finally, the chance to quit work, take it easy and immerse ourselves in the unrestricted joys of leisure. Unfortunately, as responsible adults in our middle years many of us had dedicated so much time to pursuing the extra income of a second job, or the time-and-a-half rewards of working overtime, that we had too few hours left to develop the interests in, or hone the necessary skills for, a more full life of leisure. One of the responsibilities of retirement is to learn new skills to help feed new interests. The other responsibility is to use those new skills in the pursuit of new pleasures.

There is a tendency among some of us to look back in anguish, bemoaning the poor choices or lost opportunities of our developing years, and think of our futures as no more than bland and pointless extensions of the past. But concentrating on what lies ahead is the secret. The past is now long gone, but some of the new paths are not yet overgrown. A friend of mine spent a half-century learning, practicing, then teaching, medicine. He retired at seventy, bought a violin and began his Phase 2 of life. He was a great physician and will never be more than a barely adequate musician—but he's thrilled with what he's done and anxious to begin each day anew. And that's the point—if we cannot now effectively hone those skills that had eluded us during that critical period of our maturation, we can at least change direction at no additional cost—maybe fashion a new future out of the ashes of our past. We can learn new techniques, expand half-formed accomplishments of the past, and extend our search into areas previously unforeseen or even unknown to us. It is at least possible that for those of us willing to plan ahead—even when that "ahead" is now little more than a blink—there is still a future worth our time.

Our Place In The World

In the days of our youth we knew it all—who we were, where we were going, what we wanted. We were so focused on ourselves, on the routine trivia of our emerging lives, that we had little time or interest in examining the larger society around us.

With age and maturity that started to change. For me the transformative moment was the bombing of Pearl Harbor. I had no idea where it was or what it meant, but I was old enough and sensitive enough to the changed and charged climate of our people to recognize the gravity of it. I began to notice that the world was larger and much more complex than I had earlier understood.

Now I and those other Pearl Harbor-era children are seniors, aware of the questionable choices we had made over the years, less confident in our judgment and less certain of our insights. The convictions of our youth have given way to the doubts of experience and now as seniors we have the opportunity to pause and ask again, who are we as a people and what do we want?

We think we know who we are—sort of. As children of the Constitution and its subsequent two-hundred-plus years of building on the promises of that document and on the dreams spawned by its vision of concern for "the welfare of the People" and on its democratic principles of equality for all of our citizens, we are the hope of the world and the template for the future. Sort of.

In a sense we are an amalgam of all the people from all the times of history—wise and foolish, talented and inept, selfish and philanthropic. We are the history of Man. But here in America we are also keepers of a flame lit by our ancestors—the successors and the continuing spirit of a dream. For most of us, of course, financial and emotional security remain our central focus, but the spirit of community continues to play a role in our lives, an integral part of our heritage and the essence of our traditions.

The pursuit of self-interest, of course, is a natural drive for us all, and seeking improvement for ourselves and our kin is natural and commendable, but that should not be the extent of our goals. We are more than a nation of greed and the satisfaction of "making it" should not define us. It was in the dreams of our Founders that our traditions took root, values that helped guide us for the past several centuries, but that have lately been transformed by a growing reverence for accumulated wealth and power. That is not an unnatural transformation, but is unfortunately at odds with the fantasies of our national character. And that is not who we are.

I suspect that we are an outgrowth of our origins, a people raised to honor our more noble traditions and who truly wish the very best for our fellows, willing to sacrifice some of our well-being to help the most needy among us. That had been the essence of our national charter, calling as it does for a focus on We the People's pledge to "Promote the general Welfare . . ." Unfortunately that is not an effective campaign issue. Candidates for political office won't touch it and just a limited number of our citizenry even seem aware of it. Plotting and pursuing a future for ourselves and our families is, of course, a necessary and honorable role, but as a people, as a relatively secure and sensitive people, we should have a larger and more humane outlook than simply increased accumulation.

The larger tragedies of nature—the Katrina hurricanes, the massive California firestorms, the earthquakes and floods and neighborhood disasters—grab our hearts and our charitable instincts, but the more common, while equally tragic, collapse of indigent individuals is met with hesitation and calculation. After affixing a price for remediation our thoughts turn to the unpopular topic of taxes, so our instinct for compassion is transformed into a political struggle against "big government," seeing in it an irresponsible tendency to levy ever more taxes against the hard working middle-class.

But that does not accurately reflect our nation's origins or its earlier character. In the mid-1940s, Woodie Guthrie sang that:

This land is your land, this land is my land . . .
This land was made for you and me.

This land has always been "our land" and we all shared in its growth and its benefits and its obligations. For the two World Wars and again for the Vietnam War our universal draft gave our people a sense of shared obligation, while our system of progressive taxation distributed the costs of conflict a bit more evenly. Now, our last ten years of conflict have been fought by only a small percentage of our population while several of our largest defense contractors, glutted on the profits of war, have established offshore corporate headquarters to avoid taxes.

The traditions of our nation have always included satisfying the basic needs of our population—food, health care, housing, education and other human necessities—even while providing necessary protection and support for our corporate infrastructure. In short, to some reasonable degree we were a team. Unfortunately, despite the pledge of the Constitution to attend to the welfare of our people and the humanitarian aid implied in the Statue of Liberty's invitation to the world's "Tired . . . poor . . . [and] huddled masses," it now seems a bit less likely that this land was really made for both you and me.

And that division of obligations and benefits is not who we really are.

Thursday Night Poker: A Senior Sport

Seven grown men sitting around the table, laughing, telling stories both humorous and serious, critiquing each other's skills in ways rarely complimentary—then an ominous silence. The banter dies down and an air of tension grips the group, awaiting whatever might come next. Then, throwing a big pile of chips onto the center of the table, the Dean, with a large and confident grin, makes his bombshell announcement—quad aces! Four of a kind—all aces—just about the best hand a lively imagination can conceive. Just about . . . but not quite. After a charged moment of silence, the Golfer flashes a broad grin of confidence and pleasure, turns over his king-high straight flush, and rakes in a massive pot of money.

Back in the days of ol' Doc Holliday and Wyatt Earp and Wild Bill, such a scene still had more parts to play. In those days, most players kept a gun on their lap to settle disputes or to ease the frustration of an opponent's improbably lucky draws. But this ain't Deadwood or Dodge City. This is Ann Arbor, home of the University of Michigan, and the only weapons evident are a few pocket knives with fingernail clippers at one end. And the injured party, the dumbfounded Dean, stands silent for just a moment trying to come to terms with what just happened, then slowly beginning to smile in spreading disbelief, offers his hand of congratulations to the victor and acknowledges this to be the most remarkable defeat he had ever imagined. And that is the essence of the attitude that

pervades the Thursday Night Poker group. It's not just the game—
it's the players.

The evening of poker is built around such games as Texas Hold
'Em and Omaha and all the many variations of each. The hand
opens with a small ante from the dealer, but even with bets limited to
the chips on the table, the game can soon morph into some serious-
sized pots, some of the pain of which we try to control by settling for
half at the end of the evening. But very much more than the category
or the rules or the results of the game, it is the players themselves
who define the evening. All members of the group are serious about
the game, playing for stakes that add up to fairly significant dollars
and that allow for no inattention, but for every player, win or lose,
it is primarily an evening of camaraderie, an evening of pleasure, an
evening of serious political and social analyses and biting humor.

The players are a broad assortment of productive residents
from both of Ann Arbor's Town and Gown communities who
enjoy the game and each other and represent a wide assortment
of skills and responsibilities, including a shopkeeper, a bunch of
professors, a farmer and a MacArthur Genius Award winner—none
of whom could be mistaken for a green-eye-shaded gambler. They
also represent a large spectrum of ages—from low-sixties to mid-
eighties—and a full range of athletic skills, including the Golfer in
the example noted above who is much less than an inspiring athlete,
but simply an older, retired merchant who took late-in-life lessons
to learn the game and who has progressed to the low side of barely
adequate. But he is me and I hope to improve—like I hope to fill
my inside straight.

It is not the academic qualifications or economic success or
social achievements that shape the group—it is the rare combination
of a competitive spirit tempered by a natural sense of fairness and
compassion and spirit of good fellowship. To a large extent and
for better or worse, the way we play poker is an expression of our
personalities, making the game more a celebration of friendship and
pleasure than a scientific exercise. Given the intellectually disciplined
backgrounds of most of our players, for example, it is not surprising
that most bets are made or called on the basis of carefully calculated

odds—estimating the number of beneficial cards still in the deck balanced against the potential winnings of each pot.

But poker is not all science. Even with reliance on pure logic, cold calculation and patience, some room remains for the reckless fantasies of naive dreamers and damn fools—like me. My natural and often foolish optimism has me convinced that one of the coming cards will be the one that fills my straight or flush or full house—a conclusion, unfortunately, rarely supported by fact. But it is just such personal idiosyncrasies that add a great deal of drama and excitement to the evening and makes the total experience so rich and rewarding.

While the motivation of money won or lost remains a serious factor in the climate of the evening and a prime measurement by which the night is judged, it is not the only gauge—not even the most significant one. The special pleasures that accompany the evening's interaction between interesting and interested players competing and sharing and enjoying each other's company is enough—win or lose—to make the evening less of a gamble and much more a sure thing.

And for older seniors running a little low on new heights to conquer or horizons to explore, an evening of poker with good friends can be a very pleasing experience—and a satisfying sense of renewal.

The End Of The Game

Poker players come in a full range of sizes, colors and flavors. Some are naturally cautious, just waiting at the starting gate until being dealt a hand in which the first few cards gives them something close to a promise of victory. Others have egos and/or personalities so strong that their tactic is to frighten all the competition into believing that his several mismatched cards are already certain winners, perhaps a made straight or trips or better. And some simply enjoy such a natural (often irrational) sense of optimism that despite all odds to the contrary, they are convinced that the next card will be the one to fill their house or to fit in the middle of their looming straight—thereby giving them the hand and the glory and the pot. The primary characteristics that all these dreamers have in common is their inability to learn from experience—and their love of the game.

And then there was Peter, who was none of the above—but he surely loved the game.

Peter started playing serious poker and studying all the intricate nuances of the game during his many months at sea during World War II. When he returned home he studied Law and Economics, taught classes in both at one of the nation's premier universities and became the school's Dean of LS & A, meanwhile authoring nationally acclaimed books on both Law and Economics. When not teaching, Peter spent much of his time traveling the world, consulting with other international experts in those fields, and once, when visiting Kenya, was recruited by our State Department to serve as a negotiator to free several Americans being held captive by a group of terrorists.

But always he was a poker player.

Peter analyzed the possibilities and probabilities suggested by each hand, then calculated the odds—both the benefits and the possible losses—likely with each of the several moves being considered, then bet or folded accordingly. His life was filled with the demands of his profession, but his days and dreams were focused on poker, even writing a best-selling and highly regarded book on the nuances of the game.

But as it comes to most of us, if we're lucky, Peter grew older—much older, until it finally came time to retire from the university. He kept his home, but bought another in a small town outside Las Vegas, spending most of his winters there playing poker at the casinos, then returning to his more permanent home for the spring and summer. Peter had a large and loyal circle of friends back home, so much of his time was built around them and their weekly poker games. But time does have a tendency to take its toll, so even while winning most games in which he played, he grew increasingly infirm, finally giving up driving and becoming totally dependent upon his fellow players to get him to next game (held at one of the other player's homes). During that time Peter became ever more frail, usually showing up after being discharged from the hospital's Emergency Ward from having fallen down the stairs, or with seriously discolored bruises as evidence of that day's fall off the curb, or having been victimized by some other major mishap.

And still he played poker.

But after a while his health was too precarious, his frailty too severe to overlook. He stopped walking and was confined to a wheelchair—but always attached, too, to his dreams or games of poker.

One day the game was scheduled at my house. His wife called to plead that we not allow him to play, that he was too weak and that, although she had tried to keep him at home, perhaps I might succeed where she had failed. I offered to talk to him, but by that time he was outside waiting for a ride from Ken, one of the other players. Believing I could intervene and that Ken and I could talk him out of playing that evening, or simply not give him a ride, I drove to his house but arrived just a bit too late. Ken had already picked him up and left just before I got there, so I returned to my home, arriving just after they had parked the car and gone inside. When I went in and saw Peter in his wheelchair, disheveled, bruised, confused, I knew his wife was right—he was in no condition to play. After signaling the other assembled players to stay out of sight in the other room, I greeted him and sadly informed him that we couldn't get enough players, so the game had to be called off. Peter, among the most strong-willed, unemotional guys I knew, began to cry, mumbling something about poker being his only pleasure and he could not quit, could not give it up.

It was my first battle of the evening—and I lost. I gathered all the players together to explain that the game would take place after all. The card room was in the basement, so several strong-armed players picked up Peter in his wheelchair, carried him down the narrow flight of stairs, maneuvering around the small landing that allowed almost no room to make the turn, and got him seated at the table.

The night was like most other poker nights, except that Peter needed help in seeing his cards and arranging them properly in his hand. He also needed help in calling or making bets because he could not distinguish one chip's color from the next and then had trouble counting out the proper number. But somehow he did manage to stay with the game—and as usual, was the evening's big winner.

The game was over and Peter, still in his chair, was carried back up those stairs, around the narrow landing and taken back home—where he died the next day.

Death And Taxes

As survivors of decades of battling the threats and uncertainties of life, seniors tend to be reasonably confident of their staying power—except in the face of that awesome duo, Death and Taxes. Lately it is the Taxes of that equation that most provokes and fuels continuing antagonism and although the term "continuing" may knock Death out of the running, the anti-tax obsession of much of the population remains. That popular animosity toward taxes has a long-standing tradition, but it remains an enemy to the higher principles envisioned by our Founders.

Those principles, our original guide to action and articulated in the Preamble to our Constitution, promised to "establish justice . . . insure domestic tranquility . . . promote the general Welfare . . . and secure the Blessings of Liberty." As the basis for our new nation they were designed to serve the needs and well-being of our total population—a national concept of federally-assumed responsibility unique in all world history.

Now our concentration is on the more mundane problems of the mechanics of the operation—the size of the budget necessary to meet those obligations, the source of those funds, and the methods by which they will be raised—rather than on the principles of performance. And therein lies the growing conflict within our society—the widening philosophical gap between those most deeply committed to the basic principles that define us and the more conservative engineers of government whose primary focus is on the process of the operation. (This does not take into account the increasing majority of legislators whose primary motivation is simply reelection—but that's for a later discussion.)

Unfortunately, striving for better often requires more cash and determination than may be readily available, so our noble ideals can too easily be dismissed in avoidance of excessive demands on our people. And that may well be our undoing—rearranging our goals to soften the discomfort of taxation. It violates our original promise to ourselves and our heirs, prompting a redefinition of who we are that is neither satisfying nor accurate The horror of 9/11, after all, shocked us into a wildly expensive military action without any discussion of cost—and that is the way responsible government works. And the recent disaster in Haiti moved our nation and our people to an instantaneous response of benevolence worthy of the dreams of our Founders and fully in keeping with the highly principled identity we had assumed for ourselves. And that is who we are.

But back home, caught in the torment of our recession, the many millions of our unemployed needy remain unprepared for the trauma or expense of serious illness or other of life's more debilitating disruptions. Unfortunately, too many of those threatened fellow citizens are left hanging in fear and uncertainty because we cannot agree on the best way to handle the finances of relief. The politically conservative antagonism toward taxes, supported even by many of those who would be benefitted by its largess, have so tainted the word that rational analysis is becoming increasingly difficult. And that is fast becoming who we are.

For more than two centuries our claims and our dreams had identified us as a nation in battle against the misery of inadequate food or clothing or shelter. We initiated a system of public education to teach the elementary skills of literate survival to even the most poor among us—and we opened free public libraries to help meet the literary needs of those we were educating. And we subsidized food banks for the hungry and housing for the homeless and Medicare for the elderly ill.

But now we see as the overriding problem of society, not the desperation of those without, but the displeasure of using taxes as the way to pay for their remedies of relief. It is proper that what we see as essential programs of social support should be verified as sufficiently valuable and effective and that the recommended methods for meeting those needs be efficient and viable, but if that examination verifies the claims of need, then we must act to provide the necessary support.

Excessive taxes are, indeed, offensive and to be avoided where proper and reasonable, but they must not be our only focus. Our Founders' concentration on the principles of our democracy left the specifics of payment untouched, simply assuming that the cost of honorable intentions would be met—and throughout our history they have been met. Pearl Harbor was bombed while we were still reeling from the Great Depression, but without hesitation we responded with all the might we had and still more that we did not yet have. We restricted wages for workers in the war plants and levied taxes of up to 90 percent on the higher income corporations and individuals. We financed the war effort and won the war—and very much more. And *that* is who we are!

However offensive, "taxes" is not simply a dirty word—they are a necessary part of the engine of our society. Inevitable in a dynamic nation are the dangers and discomforts of war and poverty and the many assorted tragedies of life to which we are all subject—and for our common good we must make the resolution of those misfortunes a national priority. The well-being of our total society demands that we all work together to resolve our nation's separate tragedies— because that is who we are. And of that we should be proud.

Using The Mind To Build The Body

I was about ten years old when my grandmother came to visit for a few days. She was a kind and loving old lady—must have been about sixty, but she still seemed reasonably alert for a woman her age. A few years earlier she had taught me to play gin rummy, so she challenged me to a game once again. I'm sure she meant no harm, but for a sharp and alert young man like myself to be beaten—to be slaughtered—by a little old lady of such extended age was an embarrassment from which it took a very long time to overcome.

I'm sure that gin rummy was not the only such competitive game in her inventory, but looking back now I recognize and appreciate her appetite for intellectual challenges. I don't know what other cerebral exercises she indulged in during that period of budding antiquity, but evidently she was traveling precisely the right path for people her age and well beyond. According to some new studies, such mental activity can be very beneficial and is highly recommended for all aging citizens.

Exercise of any sort is good for everyone of advancing age, but a good mental workout—whether bridge or chess or crossword puzzles or Sudoku or any other games to exercise the mind—are now recognized as mentally stimulating and hugely effective in avoiding or delaying age-related dementia. And that is a lot more than hopeful guesswork. A study conducted over a period of two decades by researchers at the Albert Einstein College of Medicine in New York concluded that mental stimulation reduces the risk to seniors of dementia by as much as 75 percent compared to more tranquil members of that age group.

Joe Verghese, the neurologist who led the 21-year study, said that following more than 450 people over the age of 75 verified the fact that seniors who remained mentally active showed the least decline in mental acuity. (In an interesting side-note to the study, Verghese revealed that while physical exercise seemed to have little impact on the minds of older adults, dancing proved an exception. Evidently choosing between two left feet is as challenging to the mind as to the partner—my conclusion, not his.)

There was one minor dissenting opinion, however, that adds even more appeal to the group's conclusion. James Coyle, professor of psychiatry and neuroscience at Harvard University, followed the study and wrote an independent view of it, concluding that there is also evidence that mental exercise may do more than simply forestall dementia, that it may actually repair damage to the brain. He believes that the stimulation of the stem cells in the brain can rewire the brain by generating new neurons—a very positive addition if accurate.

Evidently, games requiring thought and challenge can do for the head what a bicycle ride or a fast walk in the park does for the body. While some mind games, like physical exercises, are more demanding and more beneficial than others, just the fact of exertion, whether mental or physical, has an impact that helps keep the body or mind in shape. But they need not be formalized or well constructed games, like chess or bridge. They may simply be individual approaches to personal concerns. My uncle, for example, kept experimenting with ways to remember names of new acquaintances by tying some issue or idiosyncrasy to the name's translation. Were he alive today, for example, he might use the start of the Russian monarchy to recall the name of my friend, Yale Kamisar ("came a czar") or to believe that Senator Pawlenty was "more than enough" (having nothing to do with politics). It didn't always work, of course, and was often more nonsensical than logical, but just the planning provided some mental stimulation and that alone was beneficial

Such traditional pastimes as bridge or solitaire or gin rummy, of course, are not the only games in town. Challenging and interesting and instructive, too, is reading books and newspapers, or listening to concerts, or arguing politics (depending, of course, on the side you choose—but that's a personal bias). In short, anything that moves the mind in almost any direction has benefits not available from a nap or a television romance. For me, as an example, this game of writing provides benefits even beyond the satisfaction of boosting my ego when it works. It requires some original thought—making up a story or a theme or simply remembering events from a distant past— then searching for precisely the right words in the right sequence to make it consequential and interesting. So even if it falls short of its purpose or its goal, at least the exercise of its development gives it value beyond pleasure.

In brief, however we fill the empty moments of time with activities requiring some degree of physical and/or mental exertion (naps don't count), it can do nothing but good in building us beyond where or what we were—in both mind and body.

We All Belong

I was too young at the time of the Great Depression to understand what was happening, but it was clear even to my child's mind that it was a universal calamity and that it was happening to everyone. My parents, who had struggled through abject poverty, finally succeeded in opening their own store and building their own house, only to lose it all in 1932—like almost everybody we knew. By the late 1930s we, again like almost everybody we knew, had come back enough to help some of those homeless people lining the streets seeking handouts of food or money or help of any sort. The economy had collapsed, the country seemed to have collapsed, but we all shared that collapse together and joined each other in trying to mend the wounds.

Then the war came and we all shared that together as well—the fighting and the glory and the sacrifices. The draft, putting into uniform draftees from all segments of our population, built our armed services into a force representing all levels of our society. And those who had not volunteered or been drafted spent much of their spare time collecting scrap metal or pieces of rubber trash that could be used in the war effort, or by entertaining the troops at one of the many USO Centers. And those people who had managed to accumulate a few dollars over the years used it to buy War Bonds to help fund the war. We all shared the spirit and the needs and the trauma of the war—and we all shared it together.

And during the war, those who were not fighting and were finally making up for the Depression's many years of financial struggle—entrepreneurs showing record profits and workers enjoying incomes they had never seen before—accepted new rules designed to meet new needs. The most wealthy were taxed up to well over 90 percent of their incomes and defense workers had their wages frozen before they had the chance to rise. In one way or another, much as we all suffered in the Depression, we all contributed to its recovery.

And then we grew into the 21st Century—and it is all falling apart. Corporate influence on the system has expanded with the recent Supreme Court decision to allow unlimited corporate funds to flood the political marketplace. Unrelated, but following the same path, such new corporate mercenaries as Blackwater and KBR, assuming many of the tasks previously provided by branches of our military, have gained a new level of influence in our affairs of state. And the draft has been discontinued, thereby ending one of the major obligations of citizenship and further muting the voice of the People.

To a large extent the public has been taken out of the mix, a change noted and lamented in a speech by Secretary of Defense Robert Gates: "Whatever their fond sentiments for men and women in uniform, for most Americans the wars [in Iraq and Afghanistan] remain an abstraction. A distant and unpleasant series of news items that does not affect them personally . . . warfare has become something for other people to do."

The commercialization of our current methods of waging war stands in sharp contrast to the history of the Vietnam War. It was the public protests—antiwar rallies, high-profile celebrities loudly condemning the war, young people publicly burning their draft cards—that pressured the government to reverse its policies and finally end the war. And although such complex issues as war and international diplomacy and global economics should not be left to the public to decide, they are still their issues—affecting their lives and their futures—and they must be kept in the loop.

One of the flaws in extreme seniorhood is our inclination to look at the past and see what we want to see, perhaps limiting our vision to the good that was and the dreams that could still be. That naiveté may not be the stuff of historians, but carefully attended could help steer a people toward a better tomorrow. And that, I suspect, is what I have here produced—a segment of our past that may be more romantic than accurate, but which aids and embraces the image that we like to believe is still representative of who we were and who we could still be—if not needlessly squandered.

The people who made our country were a remarkable group of citizens, but to a large extent it is now the country that makes our people. And more than any other country in the world, our nation's people are generous, sympathetic and reliable. The changing climate of our politics should not be allowed to change that—it has become too important a part of our tradition to allow it to fade away.

When Life Begins

It all depends on whom you ask and the purpose or flavor of the conversation. For some, life begins at the moment of conception. For others, it is with the first kiss. Or with the accumulation of the first million (or some variation thereof, depending on the level of drive or greed). Or perhaps in finally breaking 100 at any one of our nearby golf courses. The defining moment in one's life can be difficult to pinpoint, but generally the common thread is the discovery of a new horizon to explore or a new puzzle to solve or a new pleasure to pursue.

And although the particular accomplishment or challenge or puzzle that is discovered may vary according to its essence or the needs of the individual, the thrill of the transition need not be diminished by age. It is simply the fact of participation in a new search or the achievement of a new success or simply learning a new lesson—regardless of age—that registers.

And if that first moment of a new experience or the emergence of a new vision is difficult to recall, it is easy to categorize: it is the genesis of a new direction or purpose in life, a new interest in "tomorrow."

Earlier in the day, when as youngsters starting out on the Big Adventure, each sunrise was the prelude to a new escapade, or to aspirations for new achievements, or exciting new dreams. For kids under fifty who still have a lifetime of discovery ahead of them, new beginnings are accepted as part of the game, but for seniors whose lives are often a rehash of what had gone before, there is much more hesitation to take the plunge. The fact is, however, that there are many moments of discovery and growth still resting in each of us, regardless of age, just waiting to be coaxed out of our shadows.

Supportive evidence for this thesis comes from physician/author Oliver Sachs, who notes that most people who become proficient at new challenges later in life find a special joy in their accomplishment. He uses the example of Eliza Bussey, a journalist in her 60s who could not read a note of music a few years ago. She then "trained my brain and fingers to form new synapses" and now studies harp at the Peabody conservatory, insisting that "my brain has dramatically changed"—a conclusion supported by Dr. Sachs.

Dr. Sachs then adds that, "simply thinking about an old problem in a new way, all of us can find ways to stimulate our brains to grow . . . Just as physical activity is essential to maintaining a healthy body, challenging one's brain, keeping it active, engaged, flexible and playful, is not only fun. It is essential to cognitive fitness."

And that is one of the secrets of keeping life sparkling rather than burdensome—finding and managing the next turn in our road. Aesop (according to Shakespeare) identified seven stages in the life of Man, seeing "the world as a stage [with] each man in his time play[ing] many parts." For many of those parts it is the anticipation of what comes next that most stimulates us—whether youthful problems of dating, or post-teenage job-hunting, or middle-aged parenting. It is dealing with the wide range of uncertainties in each of those stages—even in its most fragile late stages—that keeps us intellectually alert and focused on the future.

And those same patterns of doubt and anticipation motivate even the most secure and successful among us. In his 80s, for example, billionaire T. Boone Pickens started making long-term investments in the production of wind energy, while fellow billionaire Kirk Kerkorian, in his nineties, tried to buy Chrysler for $4.58 Billion. I hesitate to speculate on their motivation to gamble so heavily at their advanced ages, but I suspect it is the basic stimulation of competition, of pursuing still another tomorrow, rather than seeking a financial return on their investments that gives them the incentive to keep on going.

For those of us who have the interest and enthusiasm, but are a bit more limited in our investment portfolios, even our more restricted applications of time and energy are enough. The most irrational goals of the dreamy-eyed ancients among us have a role to play, because without them we exist as little more than fillers of space—and that is just not enough.

And that's why "Tomorrow" remains the hope for us all, regardless of need or skill or size of the prize. Because the alternative to planning and working for our future is simply to quit—and with that there is no pleasure and from that investment there is no return.

Planning Ahead

The most common complaint of my contemporaries—aside from arthritis and memory loss and failing sight and hearing—is boredom. Before being tested by the strains of age we were constantly challenged—to earn a living, or guide our kids, or please our boss. We have since outlived our job, our kids have outgrown us and are trying to guide their kids, our boss has outsourced his workforce to India and moved to Florida—and we are still stuck in yesterday's malaise.

And that is the benefit and the curse of old age—we are now less bound by the requirements imposed upon us by our earlier role of responsible adult. Retirement cannot invalidate our past performance, but it can greatly alter the routines that had long shaped and limited our days. We need no longer dedicate ourselves to predicting and dealing with events in the lives or routines of those near to us. We can now adjust our lives to once again seek old objectives and to pursue goals previously restricted by the ticking clock. In the superfluous hours of our senior years, some of those earlier projects that had been lost because we had not the time to properly prepare and pursue them, can now resurface with a greater hope for success.

Age has its problems, of course, but we need not be defined by them. Tests of strength and endurance—squash games after work, or competing with our kids on the ski slopes, or running the half-marathon—may be things of the past, but we can still respond to the thrill of challenges met and occasionally conquered. And age also has its perks and benefits well beyond being offered a seat on a crowded bus. Even in addition to cheaper movie tickets, senior rates apply to such athletic facilities as golf courses and tennis courts, excellent activities for the reduced schedules of most retirees. (An incidental benefit to those senior-rate athletic opportunities is that we must stay in shape to take advantage of them, so for those of us not wise enough to stay fit for the sake of our health, just being cheap has its own set of rewards.)

Now, with time to pursue pleasures undimmed by the constraints of work or the obligations of family, we can concentrate on all those inviting adventures of travel, or acquiring interesting new technical skills, or pursuing long-neglected educational objectives. Senior status and retirement by themselves cannot change our world, but they can make a big dent in the wall we had built around ourselves.

When younger, our accomplishments tended to be rewards of the workplace, or the accomplishments of our children, or trophies for our athletic accomplishments, but now retired from the routine rituals of maturation, many alternative areas of satisfaction are becoming available to us. Learning to play a musical instrument, or mastering a new language, or learning the wonders of a new and constructive craft can provide pleasures and a sense of satisfaction that make the achievements of old age ever more gratifying. In brief, when we reach what we had once regarded as our period of decay, there is still much more growth left to embrace and enjoy.

But senior exertions need not be focused on productive activities—it is the challenge itself, much more than the project, that holds the key. One senior friend still only in his mid-sixties and retired from his job in the pharmaceutical industry, took classes in woodworking, bought some power tools and is now turning out tables and cabinets and assorted other projects that are as beautiful and practical as making them was fulfilling. And another, in his early seventies, retired from the comfortable confines of the University and learned to play golf. He now plays in the eighties (score—not age or temperature) and spends long segments of his winters playing on courses from Biloxi to Ireland. A whole new world for him—and he loves it.

Age, after all, is not a disease or a boundary—it is a phase. I recall reading many years earlier that at age fifty-six Mr. JC Penney, had gone broke, then managed to get his act together and go back into business (his business being "Penney's"). As a youngster I was astonished that a person of such advanced age had both the stamina and the skills to start something new (or old, in that case) and make it work. And then I turned fifty-six—and opened a travel agency, a business requiring experience and skills totally foreign to me. And that is the point: Old age is evident when sizing up a stranger, but not when looking in the mirror.

Which is the essence of what I see as the least painful way of growing old. Many of the deficiencies of age are more in the mind—and the attitude—than in the design, so the less emphasis we put upon the limits and the fewer restrictions we assign to them, the closer we will be to the positive pleasures of aging.

New Thoughts for Old Thinkers

U nfortunately, those old reliable "eternal truths" just don't cut it anymore. Used to be that words of wisdom from the old-timers carried the day. After all, they've been around for so many years they must have learned a lot—they must know. Then it became fairly evident that those old-timers, now long past their prime, no longer understand the real world and their judgment can no longer be trusted. But now I'm just not so sure anymore, increasingly bedeviled by doubt ever since I joined that class of characters who don't even realize they are a class of characters.

I was thinking of that recently when I stopped the car for the traffic light at a busy intersection and saw a picket on each of the four corners, each in his/her late twenties/early thirties. They were each carrying crudely made signs asking that we blow our horn if we agreed that marriage should be restricted to a man and woman— with ancillary references to God and the Bible. I also know that such opinions are fairly commonplace and that the right to express them is an essential part of our democratic society. What I did not know (or fully realize) was my own rigidity and limited temper-control. The light changed and I was able to drive closer to the picket standing at my corner, enabling me to discuss the issue more completely. Opening the window on the passenger side, I leaned across and yelled at the top of my voice, "Whatsa matter with you? Why do you hate so much? What right have you to . . . ," at which point the traffic forced me on. I don't know what more I might have added to my thoughtful discourse had I more time, but the picket was at no such loss. An attractive young woman, she smiled broadly and yelled back, "I don't hate. I love you."

And I guess that is a pretty fair definition of our nation and our society, of who we really are. We may well be wise or foolish, rigid or flexible, limited or expansive, but on balance we are a nation of individuals with individual attitudes and prejudices and passions. And as long as we have the interest and inclination to express ourselves with some degree of rationality and control, we and our country are the better for it. I think of that girl and her colleagues with their signs preaching bias and hatred and I am increasingly angry and frustrated by my inability to turn her prejudice into love and understanding—and then I step back to reexamine my own intolerance. It's different, I know, because I am right and reasonable and fair (although perhaps not always objective), but the larger lesson is in comparison with such disputes in much of the larger world. Differences of opinion will always work to rip us apart, but only here does the abused perpetrator end the dispute with a smile and the comment, "I love you."

Which reminds me of a similar incident that took place a few years earlier. After dropping my wife off at Hillers, a Jewish-owned supermarket in Arborland, I waited in the car, watching several people marching with signs of anti-Israel hatred—not incidentally tainted with hints of anti-Semitism. Finally, enough is enough. I left the car and approached the leader of the group, yelling my own epithets at him, gaining in volume and passion all the while, until we seemed on the edge of violence. Still fuming, but drained of rationality, I went back to my car, at which point he came running after me, raised his arms and, with a smile on his face, shouted "Shalom" ("Peace").

It's irrational, I know. Certainly nothing to smile about, even this long after the incidents. But given the irrational hatred of the messages and presumably of the messengers, that nothing more damaging than noise and hurt feelings came out of these encounters, is a tribute—but whether to our system or to our people I do not know. Watching and reading of the violent reactions to disputes of similar magnitude in societies in most of the world, even the bias evident in these incidents is a bit reassuring.

I also realize this is a grossly naive reaction to a very minor pair of incidents, but this is the same guy who smiles in appreciation when he sees cars stopping to let others break into his line of traffic, or to allow a bicyclist or pedestrian to cross when they have not the right of way, or people leaving buildings holding the door for others to enter. It's foolish to try to equate the two, but I guess we have to run with what we've got—and on balance, what we've got is not so bad.

All the thoughts and ideas expressed in this book are personal and sincere and generally deal with issues of aging. This last piece, however, written just days before the book is scheduled for publication, fits into a slightly different category and fulfills a somewhat different need. The issue of same-sex marriage has suddenly become center-stage nationally and because, once again, I believe the matter to be of serious importance to the nation now and for future generations, I feel it has a reasonable place in this collection.

And, too, one of the problems/benefits of aging is the accumulation of facts and ideas that may have eluded us on the way up and may have a serious impact on the way we seniors now view life, so this piece—as another representative of this senior's maturation or decay—finds a place in this volume.

Same Sex Marriage
A Measurement of Citizenship

I didn't know him, but I do remember the talk surrounding him, the ridicule enveloping him. He was my high-school classmate in the early 1940s and I remember that the talk was antagonistic, suggesting an air of violence. I don't recall hearing of any physical abuse related to that antagonism, but neither am I confident that the attacks remained limited to talk. And we didn't use the term at that time, but he was gay.

A few years later, a friend was serving in the army in Europe. He and some fellow soldiers were having an off-duty night in the bar when several of them went to the men's room where they were approached by a stranger—and they beat him mercilessly, almost to his death. My friend was appalled, but was unable to halt the carnage. This victim, too, was gay.

Ours is a nation that has long been an international symbol of freedom and equality, but homosexuality was and remains a continuing target of derision and threat The physical abuse that accompanied such antagonism was widespread and was generally disapproved, but was rarely more than mildly condemned. Now, much of the violence of that antagonism has dissipated, but too much of the discrimination remains. As a nation of 313 million citizens with roots in all the many customs and religions and traditions of the entire world, it is hardly surprising that issues arise that attract some segments of our society while repelling others with equal passion. Fortunately most of the overt antagonism and occasional violence that haunted many of our people those decades ago has dimmed or disappeared, but bias and bigotry have much longer lives.

One of today's more vitriolic social disputes centers on the matter of same-sex marriage, with each side, of course, claiming the higher moral ground. The basis for the opposition to the right of gays and lesbians to marry seems to be centered either on a personal distaste for the concept, or on the conviction that it runs against the teachings of the Bible. Matters of personal taste, of course, defy reasoned analysis or objectivity, but objections to legalizing homosexual marriage based solely on biblical interpretation are more open to objective evaluation. Many organized religions agree with the U.S. Conference of Catholic Bishops, for example, that "marriage is a . . . *lifelong union* (emphasis added) between one man and one woman," or with the Evangelical Lutheran Church which defines marriage as "a *lifelong* covenant of faithfulness between a man and a woman." The conflict between the morality and the reality of these positions, however, is evident in the fact that very nearly fifty percent of those traditional marriages embraced by scripture escape that "lifelong union" by divorce, a percentage probably surpassed by the number of extramarital relationships tainting the "lifelong covenant" of legally and theologically blessed marriages.

Unfortunately, in trying to resolve the conflicting views directing either human or biblical commitment, opposing protagonists overlook some of the major principles that have built and guided our nation since its founding. In its chosen goal of "a more perfect Union," for example, and its commitment to "promote the general Welfare" and its pledge to "secure the Blessings of Liberty to ourselves and our Posterity," our Founders and their Constitution designed a template espousing the values and aspirations of all our people—and setting its standards very high. The dreams and ambitions of that document extend well beyond the regulations controlling the more narrow details of our performance. They are much more an exultation of principles than simply a formulation and listing of the laws of the land.

Targeting segments of our population for actions or attitudes of a purely personal nature—actions impacting no one beside themselves—or on religious beliefs unrestricted by our constitutional boundaries, is a legislative intervention strongly at odds with our generous founding spirit. And one of the more offensive of those legislative abuses to our democratic principles is the assumption by our federal government of the right to design rules on who and how we may love.

Maintaining the moral principles presumed by our nation's leadership follows no clear and precise route, but its goals of a continuing life of liberty and productive fellowship are worthy and natural objectives of our democratic system. The rules of religion are valued guides for those who adhere to the particular principles of each sect, but should have little application for citizens following a different path. Our nation, our democratic principles, are largely focused on the security and rights and freedoms of our citizenry— the individual and diverse members of our nation—as long as none of those rights interfere with those of their fellows. The intervention of rules and regulations formulated by private groups to guide the performance of an unaffiliated citizenry, however honorable, is in sharp contradiction to the principles that have built and guided our nation since its founding.

The right of gay citizens to marry the person they love is precisely the kind of rights promised by our Constitution and generally assumed by our citizenship and should be accepted as a basic part of our nation's fundamentals.

Introduction II

All the preceding articles were included in the earlier edition of this book and were covered by the "Introduction" to that edition. But the world moves on. In the months since then, more articles have been written and have been published in our Ann Arbor News and are here reprinted in this book's new edition.

And I thank you for your interest.

Bob Faber

Appearances
The Old To The Young

After all these many years of getting through each decade in order to better cope with the next, we don't see ourselves as different from our previous selves—except maybe a bit weaker, a little slower and, of course, in keeping with the supportive cliché of the aged—much wiser.

Such generosity in self-appreciation is not universal, but is rather a reaction of the individual, varying from person to person. I, for example, always believed that my performance on the ski slopes in my early eighties was as smooth and accomplished as it was in the early days of my maturity—although that may say more about my limited earlier skills than about my longevity. And lately I've been troubled and more than a little surprised when using a cart for 18 holes of golf on a hot summer day is more a necessity than a luxury—and that not even with such indulgence can I reduce the number of strokes that accumulate during this exhausting exercise. Fortunately, despite my new (or newly recognized) athletic limitations, my vision of myself as a reasonably skilled athlete, nourished by the fantasies of eight decades of delusion, remains intact, enabling me to perceive my poor performance as just another step in my continuing improvement.

For the better part of the last two years I have been fortunate to have some of my observations appear in our local newspaper, the Ann Arbor News. The justification for this privilege was the expertise on aging assumed to have been granted me by my longevity, encouraging me to give advice—or perhaps solace—to seniors entering that late and worrisome stage of life.

While the focus of many of those articles reflected my natural optimism by concentrating on the high hopes and achievements of advanced senior status (an appealing concept for most aging activists), the instinctive reaction of many youngsters just entering that period of adult status, is a bit different. Many of our juniors tend to group all ancients together as a single force, convinced that under our greying or vanishing hair and beneath our newly wrinkled skin we are all pretty much the same. They may see us as antiques diminished by the fading efficiency of brain cells worn out by decades of too much thinking, or as beneficiaries of cells grown wise and strong by their decades of exercise in guiding us through some of the more obscure mysteries of life, but in either case we all appear as members of the same extinct tribe.

The reality, of course, is that Old People are simply Young People who have aged—perhaps who have aged a lot. That does not eliminate the natural changes that attend the process of aging, but it should justify a bit of caution in accepting any too hasty conclusions. My inadequacy on the golf course, for example, is hardly a new phenomenon, the sad consequence of an aging body, but is a failing that has hounded me for the past many decades. And my poker losses are not because of my inability to properly compute the odds of success before making or calling the next bet, but are more a product of the irrational optimism that had always guided my moves in life—both at and away from the poker table.

Out of all this scientific evaluation comes the inescapable truth—that the flaws and strengths of our older selves tend to be a continuation of who we were at the beginning. Our maturity may have given us some insights or new perspectives to enhance our several strong points, or perhaps further damaged our well-being by playing to our assorted weaknesses and short-comings, but the essence of who or what we are was largely determined at about the time of our exit from the womb.

And that is a concept with which many of our replacement generation, the youngsters just starting their journey to Senior status, seem to have problems comprehending. After so many decades on the firing line and now perceived to have been reduced to the role of obsolete observers, we are seen by the young almost as a different species altogether.

One of the facts of life, however, is that it is the flaws and strengths that had been built into us at birth that largely determined our character and that to some degree shaped and colored our future. With help from our early guides in life—our parents, our teachers, our friends—and by trying to be reasonable, objective and fair when approaching our dotage, we can modify our flaws and enhance our better points at least somewhat, but primarily we are the product of our genes.

Or, in the immortal words of Popeye, one of our great early American heroes, the basic truth for most of us is that, "I yam what I yam and that's all that I yam." It is the problem of coming to terms with such limitations—thereby ending our dependence on the irrational hopes of unlikely dreams—that could be most illuminating and possibly most disturbing.

Just Today Is Not Enough

"Losing it" as a problem of possessions can be a costly nuisance, but as a reference to an emerging senior disorientation could be a definition of tragedy.

After a lifetime of working to raise a family and protecting and providing for all the people under their umbrella, many seniors grab the first opportunity to escape those requirements of guide and guardian in order to bask leisurely and comfortably in the pleasures of retirement. The lure of a life free of the demands of continuing responsibility can be a temptation difficult to ignore, so when the opportunity arrives many seniors choose to quit the exhausting demands of life in the "madding crowd" and to enjoy the fruits of labors long past.

A great idea—for about twenty minutes.

Unfortunately, despite all its surface appeal, that unrestrained "life of leisure" can be more damaging than delightful. The early pleasures of retirement—working little, sleeping late, immersion in a life free of care—are more enticing than enduring. Having little to look forward to other than more of same—without the satisfaction of accomplishment or the thrill of competition or even the stimulating stings of failure in pursuit of something more—tends to dull the days. After a life of active participation in the affairs of family and community, such a retreat into ourselves has some appeal, but can leave us lost in a vacuum of disinterest.

Old age is not child's play. The skills of survival gained over decades of aging can quickly fade from neglect. While it is appealing to just quit and enjoy the benefits that have accumulated over the years, many of us need something more, the continuing stimulus of improving the conditions of life—whether it be for ourselves or for others.

And it is that "others" that holds a special value for many of us. In a recent interview on CNN, Wolf Blitzer admired the strength and continuing activity of Israel's President Shimon Peres and, noting his age of almost ninety years, asked him about retirement. "Oh no," was the brief and enthusiastic reply. "Vacations are a waste of time. It is better to work, to be engaged, to be curious—*and to care*," adding that involvement with the needs and affairs of others is the best way to stay young and strong. "The secret of life is good will."

Peres was talking about projects designed to help some of the larger pockets of suffering humankind, but the same benefits accrue as well to working on small pieces of local community service. Too many seniors who have traded continuing participation for retirement have simply opted out of those many activities that largely shape each community's environment—fighting for a new road or against a new regulation or in support of a political candidate or Party. They have resigned themselves to roles of passive observer— and that can be damaging to their core. It is the projects of longer duration and of greater value that keep our minds and interests alive. It is the energy of staying active and involved, mostly in projects outside the narrow boundary of "self," that keeps us alert and helps us avoid the curse of "losing it"—for whatever condition that "it" might represent.

Albert Einstein once expressed his belief that, "Life is like riding a bicycle. To keep your balance you must keep moving." That may not be as profound as some of his theories of the universe, but at least it should help some of we more fuzzy-thinking seniors from "losing it" quite so often and quite so far.

Tactics: The Enemy Of Goals

Beginning in grade school, we learned that ours is the wisest, most generous, most humane nation in the world. Graduation into old age, however, is making us increasingly aware of the many variables and shortcomings in that inventory. Our Founders' denial of constitutional liberty for the Blacks, our cruel relocation of the American Indians on The Trail of Tears, the lack of legislative integrity exemplified by the Teapot Dome Scandal among countless other examples, are all painful reminders of realities of our past. Still, on balance we have remained a reasonable example of honorable governance for the rest of the world—until lately.

Unfortunately, our traditions of humanity, while fairly accurate and generally applauded, may be somewhat dated. We are the same nation with the same people, but our silhouette is being adjusted by the performance of a legislative leadership focussed primarily on reelection and concentrating more on the tactics of governance than on its goals. The question is who we are now, what are the broad goals of our society and how best—most fairly and effectively—can we achieve them?

In both attitude and performance, Americans tend to be a generous and caring people with a continuing concern for the well-being of their fellows. Whatever its roots, that sense of philanthropy was well articulated in a Constitution that envisioned "a more perfect Union" designed to "establish Justice, insure domestic Tranquility, . . . promote the general Welfare, and secure the Blessings of Liberty to ourselves and our Posterity"—an impressively high set of standards for a new nation just beginning its struggle for survival. In recent decades, however, that focus on the well-being of all our people has been narrowed to judging the impact its implementation will have on ourselves—an approach that minimizes meeting the needs of our neighbors.

As one example of many, political and social conservatives may reasonably support cutting taxes for the most affluent on the theory that it will improve economic conditions and inspire the wealthy to invest in new businesses which will then provide jobs for the poor. An improved economy, they reason, could better carry more productive relief programs for the most needy (also known as "trickle-down"). The idea is reasonable, but if the goal is relief for the poor, a more reasonable approach would be concentration on the mission of relief rather than on the politically self-serving tactics of the game.

There is the reasonable complaint of the financially more comfortable that there are limits to what can be done with available funds. Our country's treasury, they say, is already strained and our national debt has skyrocketed to record levels. There is simply no way to supply all the humanitarian benefits those liberal dreamers want to provide. We all feel badly for those most in need, after all, and would like to do for them all that is reasonable, but after a point just giving such costly services to everyone is expensive beyond our country's ability to pay.

And that is not all wrong . . . but the final determination must be made by the needs addressed, not as an afterthought to how much money is left over after tax cuts for the most advantaged has taken its toll. The argument that our largess must be reined in is not without validity, but should apply to our broader society, not concentrating on programs designed to aid our nation's most needy. Adequate service for our larger society is properly recognized as simply a fact of citizenship, like filling potholes for automobile drivers and accepting police protection and the services of the fire department without a fee. These benefits accrue to every individual simply on the basis of being an American citizen.

Those benefits do not come cheap, of course, and must be borne. And they are—by gasoline taxes and income taxes and various municipal taxes. They are paid for by those who have the means with which to pay them. The question, then, is why should these universally accepted benefits be judged differently, distributed differently and funded differently from the most basic of society's humanitarian services?

This revolutionary idea had become a bit more centrist in 1788 when our revolutionaries saw the need to embed it in the Constitution "in order to form a more perfect union [and] promote the general Welfare." Concern for the well-being of all our citizens is a basic part of our national identity, an example of who we believe ourselves to be and how we wish to represent ourselves to the world.

Obviously this brief representation vastly oversimplifies the extent and nature of the problem, but the concept remains feasible and fair. And following the path set by our country's founders, whose wisdom and foresight and idealism have made our nation unique in all the world's history, these humanitarian principles should be embraced and implemented.

Understanding and shaping the goals of governance requires much analysis and discussion, but the tactics for success must not be allowed to interfere with the humanitarian principles that underly the effort. As a nation—as a people—we are much more than that.

Our Competitive Spirit

For those of us too old or unskilled to compete in the world of professional athletics, choosing favorites from among participating teams, then encouraging them to victory with our shouts and whistles is a good second choice. Rooting for our favorite teams as they do battle gives us the pleasures of competition without the embarrassment or exhaustion of participation and defeat. We can cheer or sneer according to our mood of the moment without the remorse of having chosen badly—it is, after all, only a game. As mere onlookers we don't have to identify with the winners or losers—it's the thrill of the chase that excites and satisfies us.

And that is what it's all about—just winning or losing.

Now, fast approaching the magnetic appeal of professional sports is the drama of national political contests as the most interesting and spirited games in town. And as with athletic contests, it is the struggle itself that excites us more than the contestants or the consequences. Unfortunately, although an aggressive pursuit of victory enlivens the world of competitive sports, using those standards to run our country is a much more dangerous game. Because the primary goal in professional sports is to glorify the players and enrich their sponsor, the difference between victory and defeat is of limited consequence, but the repercussions of victory or defeat in political games go far beyond the playing field. The impact in the games of politics are infinitely more consequential and yields a much more significant and lasting impact on our world.

Those contests are an essential part of the process by which the democratic principles, as envisioned by our Founders, were to shape this new nation. The standards they set, spelled out in the Preamble to our Constitution, foresaw "a more perfect Union" focused on "Justice [and] the Blessings of Liberty . . . ." Unfortunately, in our zeal we seem to have lost the primary point of the exercise, overlooking the sanctity of "the general Welfare" and replacing its noble purpose with competitive contests to please a more limited and influential segment of the population, substituting their personal gain for our founding principles.

For a nation to serve the goals sought by our Founders and embraced by our earliest citizens, there must be an objective beyond victory for its own sake. There should be a moral or philosophical basis for our candidates' political preferences and legislative performances. Campaigns should include more than just tactics for success—they should reflect the goals of governance on behalf of the entire nation. Whether those solutions are shaped by conservative or liberal philosophies, the focus must be on the well-being of the people—not simply on reelection.

Several decades ago I had the privilege of serving on our City Council, a task to which we all devoted a vast number of hours each week—for no pay beyond the satisfaction of serving our community. Election to the U.S. Congress is an event rare and wonderful in the life of a patriot, filled with the glory of serving their fellow citizens. But they get paid—as they should. Unfortunately, they also get paid as they should not—much too often by lobbyists representing industries or businesses who will profit by their actions.

In his second Inaugural Address in 1937, President Roosevelt reminded us that, "The test of our progress is not whether we add more to the abundance of those who have much; it is whether we provide enough for those who have too little," adding that, "Government is competent when all who compose it work as trustees for the whole people."

Not a bad principle by which to govern.

Cliché

Memories from days long past don't necessarily fade into oblivion. On occasion they return to remind us of discoveries made during our periods of growth that may have changed some of our views of the world or of ourselves. For myself, one of those ancient moments of enlightenment inserted itself into a break in the action during a ski vacation several decades ago.

The Aspen/Snowmass ski area in the heart of the Colorado Rockies revels in its reputation as the Wintertime playground of the very rich and equally famous. Whether the appeal is the magic of the mountain or the anticipated glimpse of celebrity glamour is uncertain, but the undeniable result of this exotic combination of challenge and charm is that both ski aficionados and the Beautiful People flock to this mountain of gold with equally relentless intensity.

Skiing, of course, is the city's constant and overriding concern—shops filled with the tools and the paraphernalia of skiing, booksellers promoting the latest tips on "how-to", drugstores offering therapeutic remedies to those who didn't heed the "how-to", and finally the noisy *apres ski* bars where everyone repeats and reinvents the day's exploits.

But if the city's main occupation is skiing, its primary preoccupation may well be People-Watching.

Because of the variety and notoriety of the people watched—the world's most prestigious and celebrated names in politics, business and entertainment—the game is more exciting and much more engrossing than elsewhere and tends to permeate much of the day.

But every so often even such a benign pleasure as People-Watching can have an edge, a fact made evident when I was seeking refuge from the bitter mountain winds near the top of Snowmass Mountain. I had just finished an exhausting run down Campground, an expert ski slope with a "black-diamond" designation marking it as one of the more difficult slopes on the mountain. Having just taken the run fast and with a gratifying degree of grace and style, I was flush with the exhilaration of success. My spirits and sense of machismo were as high as my energy was low, so I escaped into Sam's Knob, the restaurant at the top of the lift that offered the comfort of a roaring fire, the invigoration of a hot drink and the companionship of other winners.

In short, beyond my exhaustion I was quite full of myself.

Seated with her teenage daughter by the Sam's Knob fireplace was a stunning, slender blond woman of about 40. Both her outfit (chic and expensive) and her demeanor (quiet and confident) bespoke wealth and class, another of the Beautiful People enjoying the privileges of their position.

With some words of caution from the glamorous mother, the daughter left for a few runs on her own while the mother continued to nurse her drink and warm herself by the fire. After a short interval the woman's husband appeared, a strong, tall, handsome man in his late forties. He was solicitous and she grateful. He bent to kiss her, she smiled in return and a warm, pleasant current seemed to flow between them.

If Idyllic could have a face it was theirs. There is certainly nothing wrong with having it all.

After some quiet conversation I overheard her beg off going down the Campground run again—again!—because she was tired. Could they take one of the gentler alternative slopes instead? With an assent from her husband, she asked, "Then do you mind if we go back in now?"

"Of course not," as he retrieved her ski poles from their unobtrusive sanctuary behind the sofa.

They were a different kind of pole, with a very short ski (about 12 inches long) attached to the end of each. He thereupon helped her to her foot—her left foot, because her right leg was missing from well above the knee—and using her poles as crutches she went back to the cold and windy mountain to begin her descent.

Game Of Politics

Professional football is a game—a deadly serious game. It is a game involving vast sums of money and is physically challenging to its players. It is a game that rewards its victors with a level of fame and glory that is rare from almost any other source. But despite its impact on all the many people that share in its activities, it is still just a game.

But it is not the only game in town. Increasingly obsessive—and very much more consequential—are the games of politics, the games of governance. Such contests as football or downhill ski racing may be wild or satisfying or traumatizing, but the benefits and penalties of political victory or defeat are unmatched by any

of the more traditional competitive sports. And while the rewards of political games are massive, they often depend more on "loyalty" than on any particular skill of performance. Unfortunately, when that loyalty is to the benefactor rather than the constituent or the cause we have a problem.

The most highly regarded professional team in this league is the NRA—the National Rifle Association—which sets the rules and wins every contest. They are not without their challengers, of course, mostly members of the Congress, but these tend to be untrained amateurs whose primary focus is often elsewhere.

The NRA's particular talent is in revising the rules and purpose of the game, then supplying the requisite equipment to succeed. The objective of the game of guns had always been the skill and accuracy involved in hitting the center of the paper target or in bringing down the unarmed deer, both of which which make accuracy of each shot the primary goal. But over the years, those antiquated goals of the game have been adjusted to include the new and highly sophisticated craftsmanship of the device itself. That exalted accuracy of the single shot has been replaced by instruments that venerate the number of bullets that can be fired before reloading, or the speed with which a round of bullets can be fired, or by its armor-piercing capabilities—all of which are unrelated to its earlier goals.

Their success is in the exaltation of their unquestioned power—unquestioned, that is, by the opposing team of public officeholders. The fact may well be, however, that the NRA is little more than a paper tiger—a charge made by former Pennsylvania Governor Edward Rendell. As governor of a state with the nation's second largest NRA membership, Governor Rendell, even as a very vocal critic of the NRA, still managed to win his last three elections by very comfortable, mostly double-digit, margins.

A more pertinent local example of their overrated power is the case of Michigan's former Congressman from the Upper Peninsula, Bart Stupak. As a Democratic congressman in a conservative district of gun-loving hunting enthusiasts, Stupak, himself a long-term NRA member, had been supported by the NRA—until he voted in favor of a minor gun control bill that infuriated them. In fact, they were so upset that they found an alternative candidate, got him into the race to replace Stupak, then supported him with a massive infusion of funds. But even in this conservative district of gun supporters, the NRA—with all its power and prestige—could not defeat an honest and honorable supporter of some reasonable gun regulations.

A paper tiger will not be defeated by paper bullets, but those fearful political players in our Congress might be made a bit more courageous by giving more heed to the power of the people over that of the lobbies.

Success In Aging

Old age may be restful or frightening or boring, but however it plays out, growing old is simply a fact of life—if we're lucky. Until we reach that stage it is more an abstraction than a fact, but at some point, varying greatly according to the attitudes and the fortunes or misfortunes of the journey, that benign abstraction becomes a reality that cannot be ignored. The problem is how we define that reality.

A too common perception of Senior life, at least by those only part of the way there, is a blend of bored, slowed and defeated—of drowning in the vacuum of an empty life. One of the several problems with such assumptions is that for many seniors the diminished routines and responsibilities that had been reliable cornerstones now seem slated for extinction, a loss accepted by many of the aged as inevitable—simply the way life goes. And much of that may well be as advertised, but not necessarily—and certainly not to the extent that so many people fear.

To some degree, of course, deterioration is an inevitable fact of aging, but the likelihood of it becoming seriously debilitating can be minimized by the attitude and efforts of the individual. The familiar old-age ogres are always threatening from the wings—problems of mobility, loss of vision, dementia, advanced osteoporosis, as examples—but inasmuch as those tragedies are largely beyond our control, our concentration is more profitably focused on what is still within our manageable domain.

By applying a positive approach to each of the emerging stages of life—and, as observed by Alfred P. Doolittle in My Fair Lady, "with a little bit o' luck"—anything is possible, even including an old age of productivity and pleasure. It's not all luck, of course, but an inordinate amount of it certainly is:

- luck in having the health for independence
- luck in having the financial freedom to pursue more appealing paths
- luck in having the opportunity to utilize that luck

The key point in this is that a significant amount of interest and activity still remains for those determined enough to pursue it and use it—and that depends on an attitude that encourages us to keep on going. During our more productive years, most of us concentrated so relentlessly on doing the work and honing the skills necessary to succeed that little time was left for pleasures or opportunities unrelated to our "breadwinner" obligations. A too common attitude now is that working all those hours on tasks requiring full attention took out of us all we had to give, so now we are what we are . . . get used to it and accept it. That is not true. At every age what is necessary for a continuing engagement with life remains evident and available. In his book, "Successful Aging," Dr. Robert Kahn, professor emeritus in Public Health at the University of Michigan, notes that "most people seem to feel that how well one ages is hereditary . . . [but] environment and lifestyle may be more important . . . . There's lot one can do to keep one's mind sharp with age."

He refers to "The horse is out of the barn" syndrome, by which he means that the excuse, "I've done this for half a century and it's too late now to change," is simply an untenable excuse for giving up. Changing lifestyles in one's eighth decade is not easy, so the pain of revision may be hard to manage or justify, but the satisfaction of success—even a little and late—can be a wonderful reward in itself. The health of a lifelong smoker, for example, will not be much improved by quitting the habit when in one's seventies, nor will the obesity of an eighty-year-old lover of food be greatly reduced by giving up rich desserts, but merely as evidence of continuing control over some of the challenges of life this far down the road, simply knowing that we still have some reasonable control of our lives, can be very satisfying and reassuring.

It is certainly true that in the late decades of life, the assumptions and routines of youth have only a limited role to play, but neither are they to be disdained or dismissed. Even despite the restrictions of advanced age and frailty—the exercise of a game of golf, for instance (when unimpaired by the score), or active participation in the controversies of the community—can be pleasant and beneficial. A surprising and encouraging example was evident in one of Dr. Kahn's experiments in a nursing facility. In it he had all the aged residents participate in the exercise of "pumping iron" (lifting weights) three times each week. Overall, the results were very encouraging, showing an average strength increase of 174 percent—even including a 98-year-old woman.

Participation in everything that comes your way is the key. By themselves, the more benign activities of the old are just not enough. Much better to offset them with additional efforts of both the mind and the body.

The People Of Our One
Nation—As One

J ust hoping for the best will not relieve us of the misdeeds of the
many. Among more aggressive efforts it also requires an awareness
of the problems of our people and our society and for that there is
the drama of newspaper headlines and their stories—which we have
in excess.

The ABC Newspapers Corporation, for example, noted that for
all members of their chain, seven of last year's top ten stories were
about "crime, courts and crashes," explaining, "We can't ignore the
bad things that are happening." And the editor of the Chattanooga
Free Press, when asked why she was putting "so much doom and
gloom" on the front page, simply explained, "It's what we do."

That procedure is time-honored and reasonable, but unrelenting
reliance on such reporting carries with it the possibility of confusing
"what we did" with "who we are." The headlines and their stories
inevitably concentrate on the drama and the misdeeds, but missing
is the character of the larger population whose lives are built around
the often pleasant, usually petty details that fill the time and lives of
most people. Having picked up and returned a stranger's dropped
trinket in exchange for a smile or a "thanks" has little meaning
beyond the polite, but it does add to the atmosphere that helps tie
us all together.

And on occasion some of those minor moments of connection can be a bit more than passing and insignificant.

Preparing to drop my less mobile wife at the front door of the restaurant while I parked the car an inconvenient distance away, I waited while a small group of youngsters—loud, aggressive, energetic—walked by and entered the restaurant ahead of her—all, that is, but one. The young lady, probably in her late teens, stopped in order to hold the car door open, then to help my wife into the restaurant.

The restaurant was crowded, so when I rejoined my wife we stood in the entryway with a number of other patrons, most of whom were young and also waiting for a table to become available. The benches and chairs in that waiting area were all occupied when we entered, but during the time of our wait almost everyone there rose to offer us their seats. (We compromised: I stood—she sat.)

These common, insignificant expressions of appreciation from strangers will never make the news, but they help tie together the many members of our diverse society. During the last several weeks of my wife's illness we had full-time help to attend her many needs—feeding and bathing and assisting in all the many personal tasks that are required of each of us, but which she could no longer handle on her own. And during all their care-giving activities, performing all the many physical and personal tasks required of them, they remained radiant and upbeat, continuing to smile and to reassure and to interact in the most pleasant and positive manner possible. Watching their remarkably gracious and upbeat performance under this most difficult of conditions, I asked them individually how they managed and was given much the same response by each: They had started out with the desire to do good for people and/or society, then found the job—in this case, care-giving—that fit those requirements.

We are a fairly straightforward people competing in a complex society with perhaps an instinctive drive to wind up on top, but coupled with that instinct of aggression is a continuing urge to help those with whom we interact. That is not the top of the news, certainly not worthy of a newspaper's interest, but it is a view of that segment of the population generally overlooked by headlines of trauma and tragedy. The daily papers are indispensable for ascertaining facts, but sharing moments and events—however minor and informal—is still the best connection we have for most people and their society.

Post Mortem

With very few exceptions, the articles in this collection first appeared in the pages of our town newspaper, The Ann Arbor News. Several years ago the paper's Editor invited me to write a series of columns on the facts of aging. He felt that buried in my eight-plus decades of life I had probably achieved some degree of expertise that might prove helpful to those still on the edge. I agreed with his presumption and was flattered by the offer, so for the following several years I wrote columns on aging that soon morphed into assorted reactions to some of the facts and problems of life in general.

Time has passed and—after sixty-one years of marriage—so has my wife, Eunice. And for the same reason that I was asked to write my column to prepare some of its readers for the next phase, so I now submit this single piece in preparation for the phase after that.

Unfortunately, I can find no sound preparation for that next phase. The goal in such a long and wondrous relationship, after all, is simply more of same and any variation from that is—or was—beyond my interest or comprehension.

In the same way that old age, for those fortunate enough to achieve it, is simply a late chapter in the affairs of us all, a progression onward through death is equally inevitable. At the time of its occurrence, however, it is not necessarily one that is comprehensible. Despite the pain of my loss, it remains a tragedy that awaits most of us and if there is a way to reduce the suffering of the survivor—or at least to prepare for it and limit its longevity—then that should be examined and implemented.

Yesterday, while seated in the lobby of the University of Michigan's Physical Therapy building, an elderly man of about 70—75 (a youngster by my current standards) hobbled in on his cane and was greeted by the receptionist with a, "Hi, Mr. Xxxxx. And how are you today?" The response was an equally hearty, "Great! I'm walking and doing things—with pleasure and not much pain." Speaking to him as he left the facility I congratulated him on his enthusiasm despite his physical problems and his response was, "Why not? I'm not going to let problems of inconvenience dictate to me what I will or will not do." He had been crippled by some sort of painful leg and back problem about a year earlier and has since been fighting back. After a year of therapy he has reduced his limitations, was now able to walk—slowly and unsteadily—for about two miles and was increasingly anxious to move on.

And that should be an inspirational model for the rest of us. My wife's death decimated me. I loved her and relied on her presence before she died and on those memories of her afterward. But that must not be the end of the story for the survivors. All those friends who had suffered similar such tragedies have been advising me to find new interests, to continue on. Whether I can or will is still to be determined, but what is already clear is that the fight itself must be undertaken.

The richness of our relationship continues—looking back with pleasure and satisfaction on the friends we made, the children and grandchildren we have and the memories we created. Those decades of joys and love between us will never be repeated, but their absence should not be allowed to shape the future. And that is what that old man's enthusiasm teaches all of us—work to embrace moments of the future rather than to rely on comparisons with the past.

At least, that is the theory. I'm not yet sure I can buy it.

Gun Control

One of the very early concerns of our new nation a bit over two centuries ago was how to meet the threat of a hostile adversary, perhaps even the reemergence of an England seeking revenge. Given the fragility of our infant state and its almost non-existent military might, our Founders understood that "A well regulated Militia [was] necessary to the security of a free State," therefor adding a Second Amendment to our Constitution asserting "the right of the people to keep and bear Arms . . .", a right still in effect and still protected by our nation's most sacred document.

Since those early days we have established an Army and Navy to protect our rights and developed tanks and battleships and military aircraft to further assist them in those duties. Nevertheless, the ruling of that Second Amendment allowing civilians to bear arms still remains an undisputed right.

That should be enough to relieve the concerns of the most impassioned gun owners, but seems not to be. The charge by today's pro-gun lobbyists accusing our nation's political leadership of treasonous intentions to confiscate everyone's guns, is offensive, not only to our leadership, but to the integrity of our system of government. That fear of being out-gunned by an antagonistic nation is now more a reflection of the business-oriented tactics of today's gun manufacturers than as a serious concern over dangers accompanying the regulation of private weapons. Accusing our public officials of trying to subvert the Constitution by confiscating all privately-owned guns is a serious and fanciful insult to our traditions, to our leadership and to the essence of our democratic system.

The gun lobby's contention, or more specifically the NRA's, seems to be that guns should be free of restrictions, that magazines (containers holding the ammunition) should be unlimited in capacity and that time between shots should be as nearly instantaneous as possible. The alleged purpose of privately owned guns had always been either for personal protection or as a sport, using them for target shooting or in hunting. In view of its intended end use it is a bit difficult to comprehend the connection between the love of guns and the demand for their most deadly and extreme capabilities.

Demand for the downgrading or elimination of all legal gun restrictions might be measured against rules regulating the use of the automobile. Cars, although they receive no special legal or constitutional consideration, are fully accepted as an essential part of the routines of our daily lives. Nevertheless, even with such universal acceptance, we still impose speed limits, have instituted seat belt requirements, have forbidden driving while under the influence of alcohol and demand regular physical check-ups well into old age.

In short, public safety remains a major component of driving regulations. Why should guns be exempt?

Underlying today's vitriolic discussions of "citizens' rights" and "democratic principles" and "constitutional protection" is the passion for and the fear of guns. The role of guns has an old and very colorful place in our nation's history, but in the centuries since the settling of the West our history has changed. The necessity of protecting our homes and families from the lawless chaos of that period's Wild West, or from the impassioned revenge of some of our cruelly displaced American Indians, or in preparation to forestall the coming battle between our nation's aspiring independence and the empire from which it sought freedom, escalated the gun trade to the often singular role of protector of the law.

But those days have faded. Now we too often find ourselves seeking protection from our untrained, heavily armed neighbors—and that is a level of security that can be as deadly as the crime.

The Rules Of The Game

G eriatric joys require a different set of benchmarks than does the happy road of younger dreamers. After eight decades of make-believe inspired by the movies and further fed by sensual magazine and TV ads, it is increasingly easy to dump reality in favor of fantasy, but that doesn't do much for shaping our future. The frivolous appeal of the faces and bodies of young models and the virility of the John Waynes of the West as they do their stuff on film are fun for a while—like watching such fanciful films as "Revenge of the Zombies"—but when we escape the illusions of budding maturity we finally have to deal with the realities more likely to define our lives.

And that brings us to the fantasy world of Politics.

Modern politics, after all, is largely a game and as do many games, rewards the big winners with fame and fortune beyond most imaginations. In basketball, for example, LeBron James is at the top of the list with a salary in the many millions, and in tennis it's Rafael Nadal earning double that figure—while each enjoys a notoriety worth even more in both income and ego. What they do with their victory doesn't really matter as long as it's legal and reasonably respectable—and that sounds very much like the game of politics. It's hard to find fault with that as long as the endgame is simply to win, but that's the problem with the game of governance as it's played today—the definition of victory.

From the first days of basketball in 1891 the object was to get the ball through the hoop and in tennis it has always been to get the ball over the net and stay in bounds, but the game of politics no longer reflects its original purpose. The point of American politics as declared in 1776, then detailed a decade later in the Constitution, was to achieve certain goals of governance—primarily to protect and to better serve its people. The dreams of a new nation, a new society, dedicated to the proposition "that all men are created equal . . . (with) certain unalienable Rights" captured the imagination and enthusiasm of oppressed and impoverished people worldwide. The idea of a government designed to serve the needs of all its people and dedicated to serving those needs fairly, equitably and honorably was unique and inspiring. Unfortunately, time seems to have dimmed that spirit of democratic idealism. In the two-plus centuries that separate us from those historic moments, the ideals that inspired our Founders and helped define our nation are fast fading.

It is in that loss that the values which created and for so long sustained our nation now falters and is threatened. And in much the same way that the aging Michael Jordan can no longer play for the Bulls, or that an older McEnroe is no longer welcome at center court, the high spirits and youthful enthusiasm that designed and helped build our nation has grown more feeble with age. The noble goals of community service that had once set us apart from all the other nations of history are being replaced by a passion for electoral victory—at whatever cost.

Missing, for example, is the spirit of national purpose evident during World War II when drives to collect scrap iron and rubber were community affairs and appeals to buy U.S. War Bonds were wildly successful and when the mad rush of young men to enlist for military service both united us and defined us. This really was one nation, only minimally divisible, whose goals and pursuit of those goals helped make us all family. Today's unity, by contrast, is narrowly focused on the reduction of taxes.

The Constitution's pledge to "promote the general Welfare" is being compromised by a legislative preference for the smaller, more influential stratum of our society. Concern for the humanitarian needs of those in distress is being subverted by accommodation for those more secure. Programs designed for the nation's most disadvantaged—Head Start for children and food assistance programs for the poor and housing for the homeless and so many other charitable services—are being targeted as the most convenient route to national debt reduction, in effect using funds pledged to the welfare of our most needy to satisfy the preferences of our most privileged.

Winners in athletic contests are fully deserving of their trophies and financial rewards, but in the game of politics our concentration must once again be on the larger principles that inspired our founders and sustained us for the succeeding centuries. By tradition, to the victor go the spoils, but in the game of politics, in addition to the fruits of success, should go the obligation—and the satisfaction—of serving the needs of the many.

And should that procedure be followed, the lives on both sides of that equation will be greatly enhanced.

Looking Back
A Very Dangerous Pastime

One of the fringe changes affecting most of us as we age is the additional time we spend on reflection and introspection, anguishing over our many missed opportunities, looking back with regret at the poet's "road not taken."

The trouble, of course, is that accurate measurements of success or failure are not evident until long after the fact, long after the opportunity for repair has passed. As loving mates and parents, our goals are all pretty much the same—to do everything we can for them now and in their futures—but the continuing unease is in trying to determine how that "all we can do" obligation is defined and measured.

As one example of many, providing a solid financial base for our dependents is a good way to ease the uncertainties of their future, but that takes a talent not readily available to most of us. Looking back at my own opportunities, for instance, I should have bought some of those cheap lots in Aspen before the ski craze drove them out of sight, or I should have gambled on one of those little firms with the funny names like Google or Yahoo, but that assumes more insight or luck than might attach to most of us.

But while such an approach—if it works—provides financial security, there are other, greater needs that must yet be attended and that is where the insights of age may help bring us back to the fundamentals. My wife's father, for example, once told me that the only thing of real value you can leave your children are memories—an observation that grows increasingly profound with the years.

Those early ski trips with our children, for example, first to northern Michigan then later to Aspen, are an essential and irreplaceable part of our lives. And the family's long summertime weekends visiting the Shakespeare Festival in Stratford, Canada, attending the theater in the evening then swimming in the flooded quarry of a nearby town the next day, are magical moments now irreplaceable. Even the car-trips east to visit grandparents—despite the kids' bickering and complaints of boredom—still shine as honored pieces of the past.

A bit less clear is what advice would the more mature me now give my kids and I guess the answer is—very little. By the time they would have been old enough to ask the right question or understand my probably contrived response, their inherent nature would have better advised them what path to take.

And that is one of the problems of aged retrospection: revisiting the early days of our past and reevaluating its many moments from the vantage point of our maturity gives us more nostalgia than wisdom and better serves our fantasies than our family. Because our earlier days were so filled with the necessities of guiding and providing and surviving, we may overemphasize some of the special parent-child moments that may have been lost in the process, expanding a guilt we may or may not deserve, but prefer to forget.

Meanwhile, wisdom may not come with age, but hindsight does. As antiquated survivors, we may not fully understand where we had gone wrong as parents, or even if we had gone wrong, but decades later, evaluating a distant past can be depressing and unproductive. After all these many decades, some details of days long gone are better forgotten or ignored or redesigned. At some point, after all, it is just too late to make a difference.

On the other hand, some of the more reassuring measurements of that period in the lives of our families may surface during casual discussions with our grown kids who remember with pleasure some minor moments in their youth when they and I did . . . whatever, something together that I cannot recall; or when I told them . . . something equally vague or forgotten, but which evidently left a satisfying mark on their memory.

For those of us with feelings of guilt over things gone wrong or left undone, much better, instead, to concentrate and build on what can still be done.

And maybe that is why God invented grandchildren.

Old And Starting Out—Again

"Nowhere to go but up"—one of those reassuring old clichés contrived by irrational optimists to ease the pain after hitting bottom. It is used to replace total surrender to what appears to be the final collapse—and sometimes it works.

It was 1931 when my parents, Harry and Bertha, lost their business, their home, their hopes for a future. In total despair they watched from a distance as customers came to the locked door of their bankrupted store, then walked away in confusion and disappointment. Harry, the realist, knew that the end had come—it was all over. Bertha, the irrational dreamer, didn't believe it, so they sold their last few trinkets and borrowed their last few dollars (nothing left to lose, no place to go but up, so why not?) and managed to re-open the store and begin again—surviving profitably and happily for several decades more.

But that spirit works as well in adding new challenges and designing new boundaries for people long past their prime. Except for the limitations of health, there is usually a fair degree of flexibility, even for the very old, to pursue dreams that had long since been ruled out. And it is that continuing challenge in the distant days of life that offers us the best hope for tomorrow.

In 1887, for example, Anna Mary Robertson was a farm girl in Greenwich, upstate New York, when she married the hired man, Tom Moses. For the next five decades she bore ten children, dutifully worked the farm (with her husband until he died in 1927, and then alone), until 1936 when the fragility of her 70 years forced her into retirement. That endless ritual of work and responsibility served her needs, but not her pleasures, so when she quit and had no academic or technical skills to fall back upon, she had to find something new.

She learned to paint—not to cover a surface, but to reproduce images.

She had no training, but she did have determination, so beginning in 1940 at age 80 she used the oils to capture the look and spirit of farm life—and in it found a new vigor and exhilaration that had been missing for her past eight decades. And then, despite their crude construction, those little pictures began to sell—at first for $5 each, later going up to $8,000 to $10,000 each and finally capping at $1.2 million.

This little old woman who refused to quit was better known to succeeding generations as Grandma Moses, a happy and productive woman who lived to be 101—still working until the end, finishing twenty-five pictures in her last year.

And there was Harry Bernstein who, at age 24, published a short story in a magazine in 1934—and was hooked. He kept on writing for the next seven decades, completing 40 novels—not one of which could he get published. We all know that enough is enough, but clearly that logic eluded him, so when his wife died in 2002, and he was in his nineties, he began writing "The Invisible Wall," a book recounting the love and activities he shared with his wife during their 70 years together. That hugely successful memoir was published when he was 97, then was followed by another book with equally wide and enthusiastic acclaim when he was 98, then still another when he turned 99 years old. When he died in 2011 at the age of 101, he was working on still another book.

And there is Nola Ochs who was born in 1911, worked a long and arduous life on a farm with her husband, then went back to school after he died, finally graduating with her granddaughter, sharing honors with her in the same ceremony in 2007 at the age of 96. She then succeeded in getting her Master's degree in 2010 and recently applied for a job as a graduate teaching assistant in her college's history department.

Similar instances of continuing to build a life and achieve fulfillment so very late in the day are almost without limit. As strangers, those individuals mean very little to us except as powerful examples of the magic that might still be available to us however close to the end we might be. Old is old and may often be inconvenient, but as with most other handicaps, the limitations of age need not be the final and determining factor in the pursuit of pleasurable experiences or gratifying accomplishments.

All of which brings us to that profound insight of one of America's great philosophers, Yogi Berra, whose observation that "It ain't over 'til it's over" applies as much to conditions of old age as it did in the world of sports.

Memories Of Mary Jane

In 1969, for the first time in 30 years and in keeping with the nation's highly charged atmosphere of radicalism accompanying the Vietnam War, Ann Arbor elected a liberal mayor (Bob Harris) and a Democratic majority to City Council. The town, like university communities throughout the country, was struggling through a tumultuous period of rebellion—its youth aggressively seeking new directions, demanding new approaches, voicing new objections to some of the routines that had long been accepted behavior.

The primary focus, of course, was the war in Vietnam, but an increasingly turbulent issue was the illegal possession and use of marijuana. "Reefer Madness" had by then grown from a movie classic to a community commonplace, with Ann Arbor's population divided into passionate partisans on both sides of the issue. What the older generation saw as a fruit of the Devil was accepted by the young as a harmless indulgence, not much removed from a glass of wine before dinner.

Some of us were less concerned about the harmful consequences of the product itself than with the damage accruing to its classification as a felony, concerned that by legally and socially equating it with heroin and cocaine, for example, we were dangerously dimming the distinctions between them. We were fearful, too, that the criminalization of such a minor infringement of the law might have a seriously negative impact on the lives of those youngsters as they grew into adulthood, so in March, 1971, we proposed a new legal status for marijuana, making its use or possession a minor misdemeanor.

The city election a month earlier had brought to the Council two members of the Human Rights Party (HRP), a radical group of activist young rebels whose votes were necessary for passage of the Marijuana Ordinance. The proposal called for a penalty of $9, the lowest fine for criminal behavior currently on the city's books, so presumably the least provocative. The HRP, however, had a different agenda and insisted on a fine of 25¢. We finally compromised at $5.00, which is where it stands today.

The town, not surprisingly, was split between the more conservative, older population and the general University-oriented community of teachers and students. The night of the Council debate and final vote was tumultuous. The Council chamber was packed with raucous community members from both sides of the issue, but given the political makeup of the Council, the vote was predictably positive. The community reaction, however, was not. Although the younger and University-connected members of the audience were pleased, the townspeople in attendance were furious and the yelling was long and loud. One member of the audience, for example, a very pleasant and friendly neighbor of mine, was so shaken by the passage of the ordinance that she ran up to me after the vote, crying bitterly and through her tears yelled, "Bob, you have ruined our city." (A very sad side-bar to this story was that not long afterward she became infected with a fatal form of cancer, leaving her in constant pain. I never knew the details, but I do recall that one of her daughters regularly made pans of cookies for her—laced with marijuana to help relieve that pain. My neighbor not only welcomed the gift, but learned to rely on it as her only effective source of relief. After about a year or so she did die from the cancer, but I recall her gratitude for the comfort meanwhile granted by her daughter's cookies.)

Shortly after the ordinance went into effect, throngs of young supporters gathered on the University campus to celebrate the passage of the ordinance, initiating what came to be known—and revered—as the Hash Bash, an annual event to honor "Mary Jane's" new status. And despite the size and enthusiasm of the crowd over the years, I am unaware of any seriously negative incidents. In 1976, for example, an estimated 6,000 celebrants attended—smoking, singing, partying—but with no attendant violence. And once in 1984 the police showed up to quiet a particularly loud and unruly crowd, but again there was no trouble beyond the noise.

It is now four decades later. The Hash Bash crowds are small, the enthusiasm muted and the violence still absent. Meanwhile, use and possession of marijuana remains a crime (although socially and legally only a minor one), while its use as a legal and acceptable medical treatment seems to be expanding, albeit slowly. There are now sixteen states in which the use of marijuana as a source of pain relief has been accepted by each state's government and its medical community, although the federal government has yet to take a position on the issue.

And yes, the times they are a'changin'—for both Bob Dylan and Maryjane.

Growing Older, If Not Wiser

Some Lessons of Aging

Survival skills during the early days of the Great Depression depended on a lot more than economic insights and good luck. It demanded a continuing effort to use all available assets for productive purposes, leaving nothing to be wasted—not even free time.

It made sense, then, that in order to have more time to work and earn a living, my parents tried to get me out from underfoot, so my mother lied about my age and got me into school a year early. I suddenly found myself a four-year-old innocent in a class of experienced five-year-olds, a novice forever struggling to catch up to my elders.

Then came World War II when all my classmates were being drafted, but my turn wouldn't come until the next year, so I remained the under-aged observer, envious of my more senior friends in uniform.

And so it went for the next seven decades, younger than everybody my age, until reaching my eighties when a new reality set in—the innocence of youth was replaced by the maturity of Old Age. Nothing had changed (aside from the reduced cost of movies and ski-lift tickets), but last long enough and survive the downsides well enough and there is a balance to be found. Now in my late eighties I have been granted the attribute of "wisdom" by those kids still only in their sixties, even though most of my intellectual ingredients remain unchanged. I have suddenly been promoted from "young fool" to "wise old man," endowed with the advantages of my long life's experiences that claim to have made me thoughtful and wise.

And therein lies one of the great treasures—and deceptions—of old age: the veneer of wisdom. Whatever the reality, one of the more satisfying misconceptions of aging (at least to we members of that category) is the assumption that the foolish comments of grey-haired old men are gems of wisdom decades in the making.

This is not to dismiss the lessons of life learned along the way, but simply to put them in perspective. We are who we had always been, but are now in our late years, with a bit more experience under our belts and perhaps providing a bit more material for our memoirs. What we may have learned from those distant experiences is uncertain, but the important conclusion is that we should be judged, not by labels or years, but by the essence of who we are, who we had always been—and that starts long before old age.

Wisdom is a much more complex characteristic than merely being smart. It includes a fair understanding of the rules and needs of the world around us and the will and skill to adjust much of it to the requirements of those who depend upon that assistance. And that is an application unrelated to age. Experience may well be the best teacher, but even with multiple decades under their belts, aged students insensitive to the needs of their fellows are unlikely to have learned much. Without that sensitivity, whatever designation we attach to the fact of "age" is unlikely to have much impact on ourselves or our society.

Finding and distributing the requirements of life to that segment of our population who have not the skills or the good fortune to provide adequately for themselves or their dependents is one of the more significant measurements of "wisdom" and that can be revealed and exercised long before the "wisdom of the aged" ever comes into play.

But that is also one of the great advantages of Old Age—having all that extra time to keep on learning—and trying—and doing.

The People's Welfare

Any good advertising firm will tell you to start your promotion with a flattering comment on the noble purpose and high quality of your product, but don't delude yourself with more than limited expectations of success.

Of course, not all advertising is the same. Not all promises are empty slogans designed to grab your attention or to downsize some of the troubling realities of your product. In some instances the goal is simply to spread an idea or a project that has value for those who might fall into its orbit.

Several centuries ago this new nation had just broken free from its British parent and was busy organizing and documenting a set of regulations for guiding its performance and defining the relationships between its several branches and its thirteen member states through its subsequent years

After writing those rules, however, those scholars of Liberty added a Preamble to better clarify and more firmly define the principles that had inspired the formation of this new nation. And it was that sense of morality contained in the Preamble that made clear that this new nation was for "We the People"—*all* the people, not just the new bureaucrats—that those ideals were designed and for whom the government was now being committed to protect.

And it was in that Preamble that the most broadly beneficial rules and hopes and goals for a nation's citizenry in the history of governance took shape. It was in that Preamble that "the general Welfare" of the People was given prominence as an aspiration of a nation's leadership and that "Justice" and "domestic Tranquility" and "the Blessings of Liberty" were to be pursued as national goals.

But that was yesterday. Those principles of Democracy, much like the more glib promises of cheap advertising, are beginning to give way to the conveniences of the moment. Too many of the more secure members of our population are beginning to define and dismiss "welfare" as a category of "something for nothing" and are offended that those people whose problems are the focal point of this costly legislation want everything for free.

A more inclusive and more reasonable explanation would suggest there are many people—not bad or lazy, just unfortunate—who are suffering and need help. And I suggest that even for those who may be lazy or inadequate in the demands of life, it is not in the character of our people to just walk away and watch them suffer. The "Welfare of the people" is a general term, implying a general condition of need. The particulars of that need and precisely how to deal with it is a matter of tactics that must yield to negotiations, but should not be a contentious matter of principle.

Our history is mixed, our performance often questionable, but the essence of our people is more honorable and more charitable than other nations of the world. The flaws in our past have been many and often horrendous—the abomination that was slavery, the oppression of our American Indians, the often abusive treatment of immigrants and of our own most needy—and there is yet much left to do, but to our credit, most of the more scurrilous of those offenses have been addressed and corrected.

In short, even with our economy in dreadful shape and our borrowing heavily from China, and our living off taxes that may be a bit too high (or too low, depending on your politics), allowing major segments of our population to suffer needlessly is simply not our style—and that may well be what the Founders meant when they ascribed one of our nation's most basic and honored principles to be "the Welfare of the people."

Musings On A Plane

Memories accumulated during the years of a long life can be a great source of wisdom—or at least of information upon which we might draw. On the other hand, reviewing those old memories with the objectivity of the intervening years can be more troubling than reassuring, disrupting the pleasant fantasies those memories had encouraged. It all depends on what we choose to recall and how honestly we review it.

Several years ago, flying home from a ski trip in Aspen with my wife and daughter and her family I was tired, worn out, aching from trying too hard to keep up with my eleven—and thirteen-year old granddaughters and troubled by my inability to do so. I was 83 years old and had just finished writing an article that was dismissive of the alleged shortcomings of old age—an attitude that was suddenly and uncomfortably revised by four days of exhaustion and defeat.

And that's how quickly my view of my world and of myself was changed. From simply being an older skier on the slopes with my teen-aged grandchildren, I became a fading octogenarian.

However, not for nothing did I survive all those years of self-delusion. I learned a lot—not necessarily about skiing, but about hiding or revising the truth when it serves my purpose. As a loving grandfather skiing with his grandchildren, for example, I would often come to a stop part way down the slope to watch the kids, ostensibly in order to critique their style—or to be ready to assist them if they fell—or perhaps simply to praise their performance . . . certainly not simply to catch my breath.

They may not have fallen for that ruse, but I did.

In the worlds of business and sports and politics, the competitive spirit is a basic requirement for success, but after a certain age the ability to compete effectively begins to fade. We grow older and weaker and our interests move in other directions, while the skills and goals of earlier years become increasingly inconsequential.

And therein lies the biggest threat of all. The fact is that even without the legs to out-ski our grandchildren, or the strength to hit the golf ball far enough and straight enough to find the green, or without the academic skills to effectively participate in our intellectual environment, we can still have the awareness of who and where we are and the drive to stay on target. And that is the key to staying ahead of the game.

Those of us on the outer edge of aging are limited in our choice of actions and of the skills and energies available for implementing those choices, but as long as we remain aware of the continuing problems of society and of the needs of our neighbors we can still make a difference. And the effort to make that difference determines the way in which we see our future and ourselves. At whatever age and with whatever emerging age-related shortcomings, if we can still see and evaluate the problems around us, then we are still positioned to deal with them—and in the process, to find continuing purpose in ourselves.

As youngsters, even as middle-agesters, we were competitive and reasonably confident, prepared to fight for success in whatever contest attracted us. Now, slowed and weakened by age, we are less confident, but are still able to make our mark in contests worthy of our interest.

So once again I quote my intellectual hero Yogi Berra, who wisely noted that, "It ain't over 'til it's over." And what more than that do we need to know?

Neighbors

With the aid of i-phones and the benefits of Wi-Fi and such families of the internet as Facebook and Twitter, the world in which we live is becomingly increasingly remote, adding more distance between people than at any time since we outgrew the old small town camaraderie. This growing vacuum is at odds with the more natural instinct of aiding and communicating with our neighbors and may well be damaging to our communal society.

Having said that, it is also true that much of this complaint may well be the conflict between the growing antiquity of many of our aging population (notably this author) and the modern technological skills that seem to be part of the current generation's gene code. Nevertheless it does seem to be a problem.

There are, however, ways to counter that increasing distance between people and that is to embrace some of those moments and incidents that we happen to share. Without the pressure of competition or fear of the unfamiliar, there is a naturally warm and caring relationship between most citizens that we practice almost every day, but unconsciously and in little noticed ways.

One very small example is the gracious relationship that emerges almost spontaneously when entering or leaving public buildings at the same time as a fellow stranger. Almost without thought or comment, the first person with a hand on the door handle will hold the door open for the next person's convenience—a minuscule act of courtesy that is almost always greeted with a smile and perhaps a few pleasant words and is at least a very small break in the preceding cold silence.

A slightly more aggressive effort at assistance is often available in almost any public parking lot, but particularly those serving super-market stores. One example (and to some small degree, the experience was the basis for this piece) was observing an older woman carrying two bags of groceries to her car and facing the struggle to open the door and get inside. A nearby fellow patron also noticed this and offered to carry her groceries, then to hold the door and help her into the car. Altogether it took about two minutes and no effort to complete this task, but in some very minor way her reaction—her smile and relief and appreciation—helped shape the day for each of them. All at the cost of about two minutes of time.

Or consider some of the more complex and time-consuming offers of assistance on the road. An increasingly common driving problem is breaking into a line of heavy traffic when exiting a driveway or parking lot. With slow-moving traffic backed up for a long distance, your likelihood of timely entering that line is severely limited—unless the next car stops and waves you on. And that is a favor in which we can all participate—at no cost to ourselves beyond leaving us still stuck in traffic, but only by that one car length's difference.

In short, the mini-contacts we regularly have with strangers during the course of each day—and these are just three examples of many—may help remind us that we are neighbors, that ours is a society of people much like ourselves and that ultimately it is the relationship we have with all those unknown members of our larger society and with each other that will help secure for us a society worth our time.

Hey, it's such a small matter that even recognizing it hardly seems worth our time, but in a population that is growing ever larger and more distant from its fellows, finding ways to narrow the gap and add a degree of warmth and familiarity—at a cost in time and effort so insignificant as to be unmeasurable—cannot be all bad.

Old—Until Death

The borders of life are clear enough: Birth and Death, the beginning and the end. Not so easily defined, however, are the markers of Old Age. It generally begins with retirement, perhaps highlighted by membership in a few new social groups or taking up middle-aged golf, but the conclusion is a bit less clear, frequently including the loss of the competitive spirit and the end of trying or caring—too often creating a vacuum as dispiriting as it may be deadly.

The most common complaint of my contemporaries—aside from arthritis and failing memory and income anxiety and similar such examples of age-related deterioration—is boredom. In the past, as youngsters working through our maturation, we were constantly challenged—to earn a living or impress our kids or please our boss or whatever. Now we no longer have a job, our kids are trying to impress their kids, our boss has retired and moved to Florida—and we're stuck in yesterday's malaise. We are no longer challenged—and that could be the most dangerous and damaging part of the entire process.

The skills honed during our struggle on the way up may have served us well and been a tribute to our work and determination during that period, but those days are gone and no longer have major roles to play in our lives as seniors. Our task now is to find a satisfying replacement, a way to fill the newly emptied spaces with new goals, new aspirations, perhaps in entirely new fields.

Contemplation of new beginnings at age seventy and above may strike many as a highly improbable task, but the reality is that the thrill and excitement of a new beginning in a new field generates as much pleasure and satisfaction for the very old as it did for the young.

My first realization of how infectious the age-plague might be was recalling a news article I had read while still in the early days of my youth. It turns out that Mr. J.C. Penney had gone broke, then managed to get his act together and go back into business (his business being "JC Penney's")—at the ripe age of 56! I remember how astonished I was that a man of that age could have both the stamina and the skills to start something new (or old, in that case) and make it work. That incident came back to me decades later when, after closing my fabric stores (women had stopped sewing), I tried my hand at a new venture—opening a travel agency in 1982—at age 56!

The point is that "old age" abides by no set definition, but varies according to the performer and the performance. Properly nurtured, for example, age can lift a wine from palatable to exotic, can transform casual passion into eternal love, can convert a sap-soaked bug into a fossilized treasure. On the other hand, that same time lapse can turn a good wine into vinegar—which is the essence of the dangers facing an old age without challenges to fight or victories to celebrate.

Age has its problems, of course, many of which are familiar and agonized over by those of us on its doorstep, but we need not be defined by our new limitations. With a little fight, we can avoid some of the limitations of inconvenient traditions and still have the time and interest to try new things—to find new challenges and learn new skills. Spreading our wings in our eighties can be as exhilarating and fulfilling as similar experiments and successes had been decades earlier.

But we shouldn't put it off for too long.

Traveling As Seniors

Crossing the threshold of old age may not be an occasion to celebrate, but neither need it be feared as a debilitating decline. Even "old" can accommodate most younger-life activities and may even invite pleasures of new adventures.

The most beneficial approach to the problems of senescence is to remain active and involved, but overcoming the destructive gloom of age-induced inertia may require new forms of activity. One that helps stir the languid juices of retired seniors and for which they are rarely too old or frail to participate—despite the assumptions of their juniors—is Travel.

While money and mobility are the most obvious arbiters in decisions about where and how to travel, they do not necessarily have veto power. Regardless of our accumulation of years and infirmities, most seniors can indulge in the pleasures of travel without serious concern. Although the uncertainties of transportation and lodging are troubling for many seniors, there are enough available alternative methods of travel to calm the fears of the most hesitant participant.

A cruise, for example, either as the objective of the trip or simply as transportation to some land-based destination, eliminates many of the misgivings most troubling to senior travelers and their over-protective children. By using ship instead of rail or car, much of the discomfort and uncertainty of travel is eliminated, allowing the traveler to concentrate instead on the pleasures of discovery.

And more than incidentally, the added advantage of utilizing those otherwise wasted hours of transportation with the pleasures of reading or resting or socializing with fellow senior travelers is a significant plus.

And even land-based travel can be relieved of such fears and inconvenience, because most travel packages include hotel, travel and food accommodations. For the more adventurous traveler, however, the challenges of doing it all on your own—although more frightening, perhaps more costly and certainly more unpredictable—is often more interesting.

Left entirely to your own devices you may well make serious mistakes—with the currency (misplacing the decimal point has cost me dearly in converting Italian lira), or be dangerously frustrated by local traffic patterns (driving through a residential walkway in Cordoba, ending in a courtyard from which I could not extricate myself)—but once such problems become history they are part of an experience that gives your trip substance and your mind memories.

But whatever the manner of travel, for seniors searching for variety in lives increasingly bland from the unchanging routines of aging, its benefits far outweigh most of its downsides. Even for much older seniors restricted by debilitating conditions of age and health, the potential for new interests to be gained by late-in-life travel has special appeal.

On a trip to Turkey, for example, one couple in our small group in their mid-eighties, she dependent on her cane and her husband suffering from Parkinson's, both defined the trip as "a blessing". And although not part of our group, but sharing our itinerary, were two badly crippled seniors in wheelchairs—hugely enjoying the experience.

The pleasures of travel are a boon for anyone at any age, but for seniors whose new station in life has them running short of friends and funds, it can be a valuable, life-enriching experience. The mistake so many of us make is in giving in to the negatives of Age rather than fighting back. Admitting reality is sensible and mature, but it does not necessarily require abject surrender.

In brief, although the physical limitations imposed by age are real, for those willing to challenge those limits there is also much hope and satisfaction. And even for the more frail and ancient among us, the reward of the pleasures of travel is a prize worth pursuing.

Our Principles And Performance
An Uneasy Alliance

D espite the assumption of youngsters still in their middle years, age is not the ultimate source of wisdom or of insights into the mysteries of life. As a collection of memories, however, it can be a valuable source of information to help guide us through some of the puzzles and problems still to come.

I remember the shocking moments of the attack on Pearl Harbor, for example, although I had no idea where it was or what it meant. It was Sunday morning and I was on my way to meet my friends at the "Y" when news of the attack brought new drama and excitement into our lives—even if no understanding. It was when the older guys there explained the likely consequences of the attack and let us know they were going to volunteer for service that some of the reality of the event began to sink in. It was a bit later in the war when I learned that several of those heroes—those "older guys" who were in their twenties—had died in action.

And that, too, was when an understanding first took hold that the world, our world, was larger than our family and our friends and our school. It was much later—months after Pearl Harbor and more than a decade after the Depression—that I first began to understand the people's place in the country and the country's place in the world and that the trauma of the nation were more than headlines in the newspaper, but were real tragedies for many of its people.

In the later days of World War II, when our people began to find the dignity and security of a job for the first time after a dozen years of financial struggle and the debilitating humiliation of poverty, FDR made a speech asking for patience. Seeking "heavier taxes," he pleaded with everyone to wait a little longer, noting that 'We cannot be content . . . if some fraction of our people—whether it be one-third or one-fifth or one-tenth—is ill-fed, ill-clothed, ill-housed, and insecure," then quoted Justice Oliver Wendall Holmes in adding, "Taxes are the price we pay for civilized society."

And his plea was heeded. With the people's contribution of time and dollars we were once again "one nation, indivisible." That subsequent period of growth vastly expanded our manufacturing capacity, improved the scope and magnitude of our education system and helped put us in the forefront of a new world of the internet and of space exploration and of the many other 21st Century sciences—making us the richest, strongest, most respected nation in the world.

Unfortunately, the pride that originally inspired our people and built our nation is being reduced to a collection of antagonistic phrases designed to embarrass the political opposition. The noble aspirations attributed to our Founders and earliest settlers, expressed in the first words of our Constitution which defined our nation's goal as, "to form a more perfect Union . . . promote the general Welfare, and secure the Blessings of Liberty to ourselves and our Posterity . . ." is being shifted by too many of our elected representatives to the more personal and practical problems of "re-election".

FDR's plea was to maintain the rich character and noble national principles that had defined us from the beginning—and continues to be our model.

And today, all these decades later, and despite deviation from the grand dreams that were our nation's original goals as expressed in our Constitution, the virtues that inspired our Founders continue to be our pride and our continuing goal. Falling short of the realization of that dream is an unpleasant reality of life, another one of many, but simply striving for that goal is still the best legacy we could leave—for both our children and our nation.

To Get The Business,
Cut The Price

During my years in both the retail and service businesses, negotiations between purchaser and supplier was standard practice to settle upon the best deal for both. In my fabric business, for example, I had to give a discount to the school wanting to buy fabrics for their sewing classes, and in my travel business, in order to win the contract for the proposed European tour, we had to cut our hotel and airline commissions to keep the rates acceptably low.

Such procedures are the established model for major business transactions everywhere—except with the American legislators. Unfortunately, in matters affecting the American health care system, for example, that process has been manipulated to more lucratively benefit the pharmaceutical drug industry—and its friends in Congress.

This year Medicare is expected to spend about $60 billion dollars for its purchase of prescription drugs. Such a massive purchase assumes on-going negotiations with its suppliers to reduce such costs at least somewhat. And that is the accepted process—for every buyer except Medicare.

As one example of many, the U.S. Department of Veterans Affairs, although smaller than Medicare and without their formidable clout, was able to negotiate a deal with the pharmaceutical drug industry to cut their prescription drug costs by 40%. By simply striking the same deal for the same drugs from the same suppliers, Medicare could cut their pharmaceutical drug costs by $24 billion dollars—for each year into the foreseeable future.

Unfortunately, such traditional standards for setting prices do not apply in the case of Medicare's purchases. In 2003, Congress passed a law prohibiting Medicare from negotiating drug prices, a restriction practiced by no other federal department or private firm or nation in the world—and costing us those 24 billions of dollars each year.

The basis for so narrowly limiting such reasonable efforts to reduce costs for Medicare seems to be connected to the relationship that has grown between the Congress and the pharmaceutical industry over the years. And the primary characteristic of that relationship are the legislative favors paid to the industry by the members of Congress, evidently in exchange for the financial favors bestowed upon the legislators by the industry—elsewhere defined as "bribery".

For example, between 1998 and 2005 the pharmaceutical companies spent $900 million dollars on lobbying—more than any other industry—plus an additional $253 million dollars in direct contributions to the political campaigns of the targeted (or perhaps "adopted") legislators—resulting in Medicare paying more for its pharmaceuticals than does any other large drug purchaser in the world.

As one example of the power and the spread of the pharmaceutical lobbying industry, in the single year of 2009 Democratic Senator Max Baucus collected $453,649 from health care providers and their lobbyists—*while he was chairman of the Senate Healthcare Committee*. So, largely because of the restrictions imposed on Medicare by the pharmaceutical lobby, prices stay high, the pharmaceutical companies stay healthy and happy, and our country's debt load continues to rise.

According to Marcia Angell, former head of the New England Journal of Medicine, because of the industry's hard work and Congress's desire to please a select few of its constituents, we have the honor of being "the only advanced country that permits the pharmaceutical industry to charge exactly what the market will bear"—without fear of interference by those who pay the bill.

And now, while the benefits accruing to their retirement are looking ever more secure for many of our dedicated legislators, neither that pleasure nor its security is shared by most American taxpayers—or their physically fragile brethren.

The Character Of America

Passion can be physical and love can be blind, but pride is generally built on characteristics more basic. The national pride of so many of our people says much about those principles articulated in the Constitution's Preamble and its first ten amendments, a distinction that comes not from our inherent superiority as a people, but from the varied backgrounds of the population that early joined to form our nation and from traditions established and nurtured over its many years.

Our first colony of immigrants, founded by Pilgrims escaping England's religious persecution, settled in Plymouth and soon became a model and a goal for much of Europe's abused and disadvantaged population. And that, to a greater or lesser degree, has defined our nation ever since.

Unfortunately, even as the world's hungry and hopeless viewed us as the best promise for relief from the oppression that marked most nations of the world, we were hardly without humanitarian flaws of our own. Our cruel and insensitive treatment of the American Indians was exceeded only by our inexcusable tolerance of slavery, but compared to the many horrors of world history, this new land at least offered a reasonable hope for a better future—for our own abused population and for the oppressed of the world. That dream of better days, the invitation on the welcoming Stature of Liberty to "Give me your tired, your poor, your huddled masses yearning to breathe free," gave hope to many of the world's most needy and helped secure for us our very distinctive place in the world.

Our heritage may have been the rest of the world, but we have since grown into our own people, the sum of many of the world's separate parts. Our national character was planted by immigrants who had earlier fled the established horrors of the Old World, but the hopes and aspirations that guided their move were more closely tied to the principles and values embedded in our Founding documents, a commitment to "establish justice [and] promote the general Welfare and secure the Blessings of Liberty." It is those principles that helped set our patterns of personal performance, exhibiting an uncommon concern for the least advantaged among us and setting a tone for national behavior that has helped define our character.

The Constitution's determination to "provide for the general welfare," is more than an empty slogan from the past, but has been validated by the Supreme Court as a principle defining the character of our people. Unfortunately, that American characteristic of aid for the more disadvantaged is now being downgraded by conflicting political objectives. Our commitment to "promote the general Welfare" is being lost in the dust-up of the rush to reduce taxes to make life more secure and comfortable for those least threatened. Some of our humanitarian goals have been achieved through such programs as Social Security and Headstart and Medicare/Medicaid, but such measures are threatened by our increasing self-interest in the circumstances of our weakened economy. Our Constitution's concern for the general welfare is increasingly suffering from its competition with tax cuts.

Our nation has been blessed with an obligation of responsibility for all its people, to enable them to live in dignity and security and with ample opportunities for improvement. That may well be little more than a goal of irrational dreamers, but it nevertheless remains a goal—a dream—and altogether worthy of a continuing and dedicated pursuit.

The Rocky Road Of Politics

There are very few issues of national prominence on which a large majority of our citizens can agree, but one notable exception is the almost unanimous disdain and distrust with which the people now view the players and the Parties in today's world of politics.

Conflict between opposing political partisans has been an integral part of the system from the earliest days of our founding, but the antagonism that defines the current competitive scene has become so personal and abusive that the process has lost its value as a form of mediation and compromise and is now the accepted site for battle.

Nevertheless, despite the antagonism it generates and its very limited contribution to orderly and effective rules of governance, its role in our system and even its warped performance is generally beneficial and irreplaceable. For example:

For many American cities, the residential community bordering its downtown was the town's first section to be settled and now, as the city's oldest neighborhood, is often its most damaged and depressed. In the early 1950s, one of the big political issues in a great many cities was Urban Renewal, a plan whereby those downtown slum areas would be redeveloped and made more habitable. Implementation would be a partnership between the federal government for its financing and the local leadership for its execution. I remember it being a very hot topic in New Jersey when I moved from there to

Ann Arbor in 1954—and it was an even more contentious issue here with numerous public hearings and intense political debates.

While this was going on, I met with the mayor of Ypsilanti, Rod Hutchinson, who favored the proposal, as did I. At the time, Ypsilanti enjoyed a non-partisan system of government, a fact that the mayor proudly threw up to me as evidence of the deep sense of community in Ypsilanti and the counter-effectiveness of Ann Arbor's partisan political process. "See. With both your parties yelling and screaming and getting nowhere, we, with our common concern for the community, are going to pass the Urban Renewal bill that you—with all your bellicose partisanship—can't even get it off the ground."

The battle continued for a very long period—vitriolic, often irrational and joined by just about every civic and social organization in town. Ann Arbor did finally get it off the ground and passed a seriously watered down version of what had originally been proposed, while Ypsilanti, with its generally uncontested acceptance of the wisdom of the proposal, got nowhere. Mayor Hutchinson and I were both surprised by the bill's defeat in Ypsilanti, finally concluding that, although they had no organized opposition, neither did they have any effective organized support . . . so it simply died from disinterest.

The message that we both took away from this was that political partisanship can be ugly and is often irrational and destructive, but with it we have passion and the likelihood of some level of performance, while without it we too often have a vacuum of disinterest and inaction.

It is probably true that in an ideal world, good solutions to complex problems—even while dividing proponents with opposing views—are in the compromises reached between their honest representatives. But the world of politics seems to follow a different path. The mechanics of the democratic system of government may well be outside our preferred style of operation, but if that's the only game in town we have no choice but to make it work.

And that requires an active and continuing citizen participation in community affairs. We cannot assign responsibilities to others, then simply walk away. The nation is ours, the local community is ours—the decisions must be ours.

For a number of reasons, including the insights and objectivity that at least occasionally come with age, we seniors must remain involved—but, in addition to the well-being of society, for reasons more personal and unrelated to the welfare of the community. As seniors grow ever older, we tend to become increasingly sedentary, giving in to the accepted assumption of non-productive time-filling—almost a guarantee of more rapid deterioration.

An active engagement of seniors with the affairs of their community, in addition to the hope of improving the lives of its people, includes the advantage of providing a beneficial alternative activity for too frequently bored and inactive seniors. Thoughtful and productive participation in the affairs of others, beyond the satisfaction of aiding our neighbors, can give us a little more time and a lot more end-of-life interest.

New Paths To The Future
Minimize The Tactics—
Emphasize The Goals

D espite the limited evidence of principles directing the game of Politics, it remains the only acceptable route to democratic governance, so—whatever its problems—we have to make it work. Unfortunately, with so many of its players being courted and supported by goals and a constituency forever focussed on the next election, the system is now more the tactics of the process than its humanitarian goals—a serious blow to the higher moral standards we had once believed were ours.

As a nation whose founding purpose was "to form a more perfect Union" and whose pledge was "to promote the general Welfare," there is a rich humanitarian tradition attached to our existence— one that is now at odds with much of our current performance. That original commitment to serve the needy of our society, for example, is a tribute to the essence of who we are and have been since our founding, but the likelihood of carrying those responsibilities forward into continuing generations is increasingly sidelined by the tactics chosen for the task—a condition known as "taxes".

There is, of course, the complaint of those less needy (in effect, those who would foot the bill) who insist that we simply cannot afford the costs of supporting those who have not the means to do for themselves. Because they see as our first priority the restoration of our country's economy, they advocate holding off subsidizing many of our national aid programs until the economy improves– a commendable goal as long as the cost of that economic repair is in keeping with the principles that define us. Such an approach in regard to medical treatment, for example, would make more sense if we could also hold off the damaging effects of untreated health problems for that same period. Unfortunately, the damages to the human health system that may result from inattention cannot always be corrected after their onset—which makes the tactic of delay very dangerous.

It is true that a generous nation can do more good for its people when its economy is strong, but the projects themselves must not be sacrificed to that cause. One of the tactics now being pursued in the name of national well-being, for example, is to improve the fiscal health of those industries whose success will likely result in increased employment—an unquestionably commendable goal. Nevertheless, if pursued too aggressively and with a concentration too narrowly focused on the needs and demands of industry, the implementation of such an approach could be very dangerous for our larger society.

For example, in order to pay for the project, Meals On Wheels, a federal program providing needed nutrients to indigent seniors since 1972, is now facing budget cuts that will eliminate many millions of meals from its program.

And at the other end of the age scale, funds to keep the airlines working efficiently is planned to be paid by budget cuts for Head Start, causing 70,000 children to lose access to that program— during this most critical period in their short lives.

We all applaud building a stronger economy, but the core humanitarian projects dependent on that economy must not be sacrificed to that cause. Federally financed programs providing valuable assistance to the needy are obligations to the people of the nation no less valid than reducing the burdens of taxation may be for those who pay such taxes. However disconnected the privileged and the needy are from each other, the nation—with *all* its benefits and *all* its problems—belongs to *all* its people.

In short, our primary focus should be on the target—not the tactics.

The Principles Of Governance

The flaws and misdeeds in our nation's past—such scandals as Teapot Dome and Watergate and far beyond—have left black marks on our history that can be troubling to the citizens of today, but having overcome so many of those flaws might also be a source of pleasure and pride.

We began, after all, as the refuge for abused people of the world, first providing sanctuary to the oppressed citizens of Spain in the16th century, then to the Huguenots escaping religious persecution. The aid they sought and found in this new land of America was later formalized by a Declaration Of Independence that declared that "all men are created equal . . . with certain unalienable Rights". That was the beginning of a whole new era, unique in the history of Man, in which the citizen became the focus and the purpose of government.

And right from that beginning it worked. Washington Irving, even with his deep love of all things British, had to concede that the United States was "a country in a singular state of moral and physical development; a country in which one of the greatest Political experiments in the history of the world is now performing."

And that is who once we were. Since then, our pride as a nation sworn to "promote the general Welfare" has redirected its attention from "the welfare of the people" to programs largely centered on avoidance of taxes. The idealism conceived in a spirit of purity of purpose and with the well-being of our fellows as its central focus, is being transformed into personal struggles of self-interest.

Unfortunately, our national focus is increasingly about the tactics of governance rather than the goals or ideals that motivated our Founders and inspired our earliest settlers. Our drive is no longer about what we want as a nation—it is about how much we are willing to pay for it and the least inconvenient way to find the funds. The looming tragedy of cutting back on food stamps to feed the most needy is a good example of our nation's current concentration on easing the burden of taxation rather than improving the lives of our people.

In the several centuries since our founding, our nation has changed—grown older and stronger and richer. But while "the prevalence of sound moral and religious principles" so vigorously lauded by Washington Irving is still there, it has lost much of its blossom.

And with that maturity our character is changing as well as our profile. What once was praised as "one of the greatest Political experiments in the history of the world" is now fading, giving way to some of the same sins of insensitivity that had originally encouraged the founding of our nation. Tax relief as both a tactic and a prize is properly of serious interest to us all, but should not be central to our performance or define our goals.

The noble principles expressed in the Preamble to our Constitution—to "establish Justice . . . promote the general Welfare . . . secure the Blessings of Liberty . . ."—are being reduced to quaint slogans of little consequence. However short of its apparent reality, we really are a nation of idealism, conceived and fashioned in a spirit of purity of purpose. Our achievements, of course, will never reach the glory of our dreams, but those aspirations of our earliest settlers should still be the principles by which we strive to govern.

And even if that reverie is no more solid than Don Quixote's "impossible dream" we are still that much further ahead simply for having set goals a bit higher than "tax reduction" and is a whole lot closer to who we really are—as both a nation and a people.

CPSIA information can be obtained
at www.ICGtesting.com
Printed in the USA
LVHW090022100619
620620LV00012BA/1076/P